THE *Red Hat Society*.
DESSERT COOKBOOK

~

Eat Dessert First!

INTRODUCTIONS BY SUE ELLEN COOPER

EDITED BY CAROL BOKER

PHOTOGRAPHS BY ERIK BOKER

THOMAS NELSON
Since 1798

NASHVILLE   DALLAS   MEXICO CITY   RIO DE JANEIRO   BEIJING

07 Dec7
3+T
2499(387)

Published in Nashville, Tennessee, by Thomas Nelson. Thomas Nelson is a trademark of Thomas Nelson, Inc.

Thomas Nelson, Inc. titles may be purchased in bulk for educational, business, fund-raising, or sales promotional use. For information, please e-mail SpecialMarkets@ThomasNelson.com.

Photo styling and testing by Victoria Storm

Library of Congress Cataloging-in-Publication Data

Eat dessert first! / The Red Hat Society ; introductions by Sue Ellen Cooper ; photographs by Erik Boker.
    p. cm.
  Includes bibliographical references and index.
  ISBN 978-1-4016-0363-2
  1. Desserts. 2. Baking. I. Cooper, Sue Ellen. II. Red Hat Society.
TX773.E3193 2007
641.8'6—dc22   2007023174

Printed in the United States of America

07 08 09 10 11 12—5 4 3 2 1

Contents

Introduction

It is said that the ability to accept and apply the principle of delayed gratification is a sign that a person has reached adulthood. Most of us start learning this principle early. No matter how old you are now, there's a good likelihood that you have heard (and made) statements like these, some time in your life:

"Finish your homework before you turn on the TV."

"Finish your chores before you go outside to play."

"Finish your vegetables before you ask for dessert."

Conventional wisdom dictates that the hard part has to come first; then—and *only* then—the pay-off follows. We even structure our meals on this model. The Merriam-Webster dictionary defines "dessert" as "a usually sweet course or dish (as of pastry or ice cream) usually served at the end of a meal."

But, here's some food for thought (sorry, I never could resist a pun). I recently ran across this anonymous quotation: "The best part of dinner is the dessert, and it usually arrives when you can't eat any more."

That puts things in a whole new light, don't you think? Now that we're independent, oh-so-mature adults, who can tell us that we can't occasionally reverse the principle of delayed gratification? Wouldn't a creamy wedge of cheesecake taste even better if you dug into it when you were *really* hungry, instead of stuffing it down after you're already sated? Wouldn't your "inner child" think she was *really* getting away with something? Wouldn't it be FUN? We Red Hat Society members think so! And, if you need it, we even give you our permission to (at least occasionally) eat dessert first!

Sue Ellen Cooper, Exalted Queen Mother

Red Hat Society

Cakes for Every Occasion

Birthdays, holidays, society luncheons—always a reason (or who needs a reason) to celebrate.

There's an old song that begins, "If I knew you were comin', I'd have baked a cake . . ." The ever-popular cake has become a sign of both celebration and hospitality. With or without candles, a cake is a familiar, homey treat. This type of dessert may be common, but the list of potential ingredients is long. Included in the following recipes are such diverse ingredients as fruit (apples, strawberries, prunes), vegetables (potatoes, carrots), chocolate, whiskey, nuts—even lavender! With all these choices, at least one of these recipes is bound to become your favorite!

Raw Apple Cake

2   large eggs
2   cups sugar
2/3 cup canola oil
4   cups shredded, peeled apples
3   cups all-purpose flour
2   teaspoons baking soda

2   teaspoons cinnamon
1   cup chopped nuts
1   cup chopped raisins
2   teaspoons vanilla
    Confectioners' sugar

Preheat the oven to 350 degrees. Grease and flour a 13 x 9-inch baking pan. Set aside.

In a large bowl beat the eggs until fluffy. Add the sugar and oil. Stir in the apples.

In a medium bowl combine the flour, baking soda, and cinnamon. Add to the apple mixture. Stir in the nuts, raisins, and vanilla. Mix well. Pour into the prepared pan, and bake 35 to 40 minutes, or until a knife inserted in the center comes out clean. Cool on a wire rack. Dust with confectioners' sugar before serving.

Makes 10 to 12 servings

Carol Betush, Queen
Rebellious Elegant Dames,
Redding, California

Apple Cake with Cream Cheese Icing

CAKE BATTER:

- 2 large eggs
- 2 cups sugar
- 1/2 cup vegetable oil
- 1 teaspoon vanilla
- 2 cups all-purpose flour
- 1/2 teaspoon salt
- 1 teaspoon baking soda
- 2 teaspoons cinnamon
- 1/4 teaspoon nutmeg
- 4 cups peeled and diced apples
- 1 cup chopped walnuts

ICING:

- 1 (3-ounce) package cream cheese, softened
- 3 tablespoons butter, softened
- Pinch of salt
- 1/2 teaspoon vanilla
- 1 1/2 cups confectioners' sugar

Preheat the oven to 350 degrees. Grease and flour a 13 x 9-inch baking pan. Set aside.

For the cake, in a large bowl beat the eggs until light and fluffy. Gradually add the sugar, oil, and vanilla. Add the flour, salt, baking soda, cinnamon, and nutmeg. (The batter will be stiff.) Stir in the apples and walnuts. Spoon the batter into the prepared pan. Bake 40 minutes. Cool in the pan 15 minutes. Remove from the pan and place on a serving plate.

For the icing, combine the cream cheese, butter, salt, vanilla, and confectioners' sugar in a medium bowl. Beat with an electric mixer until smooth. Frost the cooled cake.

Makes 10 to 12 servings

Paula Rae Espy, Red Hat Accountess
Red Hot River Babes,
Burlington, Iowa

Best-Ever Coconut Pound Cake

CAKE BATTER:
- 5 large eggs, beaten
- 2 cups sugar
- 1 cup vegetable oil
- 2 cups all-purpose flour
- 1/4 teaspoon salt
- 1 1/2 teaspoons baking powder
- 1/4 cup milk
- 1 teaspoon vanilla
- 1 teaspoon coconut extract
- 1 cup flaked coconut

GLAZE:
- 2 cups sugar
- 1 cup milk
- 1/2 cup (1 stick) butter

Preheat the oven to 325 degrees. Grease and flour a 10-inch tube pan. Set aside.

For the cake, in a large bowl combine the eggs, sugar, and oil, mixing well.

In a medium bowl combine the flour, salt, and baking powder. Stir into the egg mixture, beating lightly. Add the milk, vanilla, coconut extract, and the coconut. Mix thoroughly. Pour into the prepared pan. Bake 1 hour, or until a wooden pick inserted in the center of the cake comes out clean. Remove from the oven, loosen the cake from the edge of the pan with a knife, and prick the top of the cake in several places with a toothpick.

For the glaze, in a small saucepan combine the sugar, milk, and butter over medium heat. Cook until the sugar dissolves, stirring constantly. Pour the mixture over the hot cake. Cool the cake in the pan before removing to a serving plate. This cake freezes well.

Makes 16 servings

Karon Saul, Queen Mum
Wacky Women of The Ya Ya Sisterhood,
Jacksonville, Florida

Aunt Edna's Christmas Cake

3 large apples, peeled and sliced	3/4 cup granulated sugar
1 cup chocolate chips, divided	2 large eggs
1 cup chopped nuts, divided	1 teaspoon baking powder
2 1/2 cups all-purpose flour, divided	1 teaspoon baking soda
1/2 cup shortening	1/2 teaspoon salt
1 1/4 cups firmly packed brown sugar, divided	1 cup cold water
	1 teaspoon vanilla

Preheat the oven to 350 degrees. Grease a 13 x 9-inch baking pan. Set aside.

In a medium bowl combine the apples, 1/2 cup of the chocolate chips, 1/2 cup of the chopped nuts, and 1/2 cup of the flour. Toss together to coat the mixture and set aside.

In a large bowl cream the shortening, 3/4 cup of the brown sugar, the granulated sugar, and eggs. Add the remaining 2 cups of the flour, the baking powder, baking soda, and salt alternately with the cold water and vanilla. Mix well. Fold in the apple mixture. Spread into the prepared pan.

In a small bowl mix the remaining 1/2 cup brown sugar, the remaining 1/2 cup chocolate chips, and the remaining 1/2 cup nuts together and sprinkle on top of the batter. Bake 30 to 45 minutes, or until a toothpick inserted in the center comes out clean.

Makes 24 servings

Patricia Ruegger, Queen Mother

Winter Flakes,
Ojibwa, Wisconsin

Low-Fat Blueberry Pound Cake

Cooking spray
2 cups sugar
1/2 cup (1 stick) light butter
4 ounces reduced fat cream cheese, softened
3 large eggs
1 large egg white
3 cups all-purpose flour, divided
2 cups fresh or frozen blueberries

1 teaspoon baking powder
1/2 teaspoon baking soda
1/2 teaspoon salt
1 (8-ounce) container low-fat lemon yogurt
2 teaspoons vanilla extract
1/2 cup confectioners' sugar
4 teaspoons lemon juice

Preheat the oven to 350 degrees. Spray a 10-inch tube pan with cooking spray. Set aside.

In a large bowl beat the sugar, butter, and cream cheese at medium speed with an electric mixer for 5 minutes, or until well blended. Add the eggs, one at a time, beating well after each addition. Add the egg white. Mix well.

In a small bowl combine 2 tablespoons of the flour and the blueberries. Toss well. In a medium bowl, combine the remaining flour, the baking powder, baking soda, and salt. Add the flour mixture to the sugar mixture alternately with the yogurt, beginning and ending with the flour mixture. Fold in the blueberry mixture and the vanilla.

Pour the cake batter into the prepared pan. Bake 1 hour and 10 minutes, or until a wooden pick inserted in the center comes out clean. Cool the cake in the pan 10 minutes. Remove from the pan.

In a small bowl combine the confectioners' sugar and the lemon juice. Drizzle the mixture over the warm cake. Cut with a serrated knife.

Makes 16 servings

Claire Knodell, *Munkus the Brat*

Red Hot Jazzy Ladies,
Kelowna, British Columbia

Peach Pound Cake

1 cup (2 sticks) butter, softened	3 cups all-purpose flour
3 cups sugar	1/4 teaspoon baking soda
6 large eggs, at room temperature	1/2 teaspoon salt
1 teaspoon vanilla extract	1/2 cup sour cream
1/2 teaspoon almond extract	2 cups peeled chopped peaches

Preheat the oven to 350 degrees. Grease and flour a 10-inch tube pan. Set aside.

In a large mixing bowl cream the butter and sugar until light and fluffy. Add the eggs, one at a time, beating after each addition. Stir in the vanilla and almond extracts.

In a medium bowl combine the flour, baking soda, and salt. Add to the creamed mixture, 1 cup at a time, stirring well after each addition. Fold in the sour cream and peaches. Pour into the prepared pan. Bake 75 to 85 minutes, or until a toothpick inserted in the center comes out clean. Cool in the pan on a wire rack.

Makes 16 servings

Fran Pritchert, Vice Queen
Scarlet Sophisticates,
Woodbridge, Virginia

Sweet Potato Pound Cake

1 cup (2 sticks) margarine, softened	1 teaspoon baking soda
2 cups sugar	1 teaspoon ground cinnamon
4 large eggs	1/2 teaspoon ground nutmeg
2 1/2 cups cooked, mashed sweet potatoes (about 4 to 5 medium)	1/4 teaspoon salt
3 cups all-purpose flour	1 teaspoon vanilla
2 teaspoons baking powder	1/2 cup flaked coconut
	1/2 cup chopped pecans

Preheat the oven to 350 degrees. Grease a 10-inch tube pan. Set aside.

In a large bowl cream the margarine. Gradually add the sugar, beating well. Add the eggs, one at a time, beating well after each addition. Add the sweet potatoes, beating well.

In a medium bowl combine the flour, baking powder, baking soda, cinnamon, nutmeg, and salt. Gradually add to the sweet potato mixture, beating well after each addition (batter will be stiff). Stir in the vanilla, coconut, and pecans.

Spoon the batter into the prepared pan. Bake 1 hour, or until a wooden pick inserted in the center comes out clean. Cool in the pan for 15 minutes. Remove from the pan and let cool completely.

Makes 10 to 12 servings

Dianne Buehrer, Countess Double Delight
Ramblin' Red Roses,
Canton, Ohio

Peanut Butter Sheet Cake

CAKE BATTER:

- 2 cups sugar
- 2 cups all-purpose flour
- 2 large eggs
- 1 teaspoon baking soda
- 1 cup sour cream
- 2/3 cup creamy or crunchy peanut butter
- 1 cup (2 sticks) butter or margarine
- 1 cup water

ICING:

- 1/2 cup (1 stick) butter or margarine
- 2/3 cup creamy or crunchy peanut butter
- 6 tablespoons milk
- 2 1/2 cups confectioners' sugar
- 1 teaspoon vanilla

Preheat the oven to 400 degrees.

For the cake, in a large bowl combine the sugar and flour, and set aside.

In a medium bowl mix the eggs, baking soda, and sour cream. Set aside. In a small saucepan combine the peanut butter, butter, and water. Bring to a boil. Add the boiled mixture to the flour mixture. Stir in the sour cream mixture. Pour into a 15 x 10-inch sheet cake pan and bake 20 minutes, or until a wooden pick inserted in the center comes out clean.

For the icing, combine the butter, peanut butter, and milk in a medium saucepan. Bring to a boil, stirring constantly. Add the confectioners' sugar and the vanilla. Stir until thickened and pour over the cake while still warm.

Makes 20 servings

Maureen Williams, Marquessa of Enchantment

Dusty Desert Roses,
Desert Hot Springs, California

Prune Cake

CAKE BATTER:

- 1   cup shortening or oil
- 2   cups sugar
- 1   cup buttermilk
- 3   large eggs
- 2   cups all-purpose flour
- 1   teaspoon baking soda
- 1/2   teaspoon salt
- 1   teaspoon each allspice, nutmeg, cinnamon, and cloves
- 1   teaspoon vanilla
- 1/2   cup chopped nuts
- 1 1/2   cups chopped prunes

CARAMEL ICING:

- 1/2   cup (1 stick) butter
- 1   (16-ounce) box brown sugar
- 1/2   teaspoon vanilla
- 1/2   (5-ounce) can evaporated milk
- 4   cups confectioners' sugar

Preheat the oven to 350 degrees. Grease and flour a 10-inch tube pan. Set aside.

For the cake, in a large bowl mix the shortening, sugar, buttermilk, and eggs. In a medium bowl combine the flour, baking soda, salt, and spices. Gradually add the dry ingredients to the creamed mixture. Add the vanilla and then fold in the nuts and prunes. Pour into the prepared pan. Bake 50 to 60 minutes.

For the icing, melt the butter in a large saucepan over medium heat. Stir in the brown sugar. Continue stirring for 5 minutes. Add the vanilla and evaporated milk. Remove from the heat and quickly beat in the confectioners' sugar until reaching the desired spreading consistency. (If the mixture is too thick, add more milk.) Spread over the cake.

Makes 20 servings

Rosa Floyd, Regal Rosa
Blue Grass Red Hat Society,
Lexington, Kentucky

Belle Goodfriend's Date-Nut Cake

1 cup chopped dates, solidly packed	1/8 teaspoon salt
1/2 cup chopped walnuts	1 cup sugar
1 cup boiling water	1/2 cup (1 stick) butter, softened
1 cup all-purpose flour	2 large eggs
3/4 cup whole-wheat flour	1 teaspoon vanilla extract
1/2 teaspoon baking powder	Whipped topping or whipped cream, for garnish
1 teaspoon baking soda	

Preheat the oven to 350 degrees. Grease and flour a 13 x 9-inch baking pan. Set aside.

In a small bowl combine the dates, walnuts, and water. Let stand until cooled.

In a medium bowl combine the flours, baking powder, baking soda, and salt. In a large bowl cream together the sugar and butter. Add the eggs and beat well to combine. Stir in the date-nut mixture. Add the flour mixture to the wet mixture, beating just until combined. Add the vanilla and beat well. Pour into the prepared baking pan and bake 20 to 30 minutes, or until a toothpick inserted in the center comes out clean. Serve warm or at room temperature with whipped topping.

Makes 16 servings

Joanne Harter, Lady HiJinks, Court Jester

*Hot Tamales of Watertown,
Harrisville, New York*

Cranberry Cake with Hot Butter Sauce

CAKE BATTER:

- 2 tablespoons butter, melted
- 1 cup sugar
- 1 teaspoon vanilla
- 2 cups all-purpose flour
- 3 teaspoons baking powder
- 1/2 teaspoon salt
- 1 cup milk
- 2 cups fresh cranberries

HOT BUTTER SAUCE:

- 1/2 cup (1 stick) butter
- 1 cup sugar
- 1/2 cup half-and-half

Preheat the oven to 400 degrees. Grease an 8 x 8-inch or 9 x 9-inch pan. Set aside.

For the cake, in a large bowl cream the butter and sugar with an electric mixer. Add the vanilla.

In a medium bowl combine the flour, baking powder, and salt. Add the flour mixture and milk alternately to the butter mixture and mix thoroughly. Fold in the cranberries. Pour the batter into the prepared pan. Bake 30 to 35 minutes or until a toothpick inserted into the center comes out clean.

For the hot butter sauce, in a small saucepan melt the butter and blend in the sugar. Stir in the half-and-half. Simmer 3 to 4 minutes, stirring occasionally.

While the cake is still warm, cut into squares and top with the hot butter sauce.

Makes 8 to 10 servings

JoAnne Badger, Member
Mainely Madams,
Turner, Maine

Double-Delicious Banana Cake

6 large bananas, divided	1 tablespoon lemon juice
1 (16-ounce) package pound cake mix	1 cup (2 sticks) butter, softened
2 large eggs	1 (16-ounce) package confectioners' sugar
1 cup milk, divided	1 tablespoon vanilla

Preheat the oven to 350 degrees. Grease and flour three 9-inch round cake pans. Set aside.

In a large bowl mash 3 of the bananas. Add the cake mix, eggs, and 1/3 cup of the milk, mixing well. Spoon the batter evenly into the prepared pans and bake 20 minutes or until a wooden pick inserted in the center comes out clean. Cool.

Slice the remaining 3 bananas. Place in a medium bowl and toss with lemon juice. Drain on paper towels. Using the same bowl, combine the butter, confectioners' sugar, the remaining 2/3 cup milk, and the vanilla. Mix until creamy. Spread the icing on top of one cake layer and top with one-third of the banana slices. Repeat with the remaining layers, spreading the remaining icing on the top and side of the cake.

Makes 15 servings

Angela Vitale, Lady Sweet Pea Sagittaria
Sophisticated Red Hat Ladies,
Auburn, New York

Strawberry Dreamy Cream Cake

1 baked angel food cake

2 quarts fresh strawberries

1 (3.4-ounce) package instant vanilla pudding

1 (20-ounce) can crushed pineapple, undrained

1 (8-ounce) container frozen whipped topping, thawed

Cut the angel food cake into 3 layers. Slice the strawberries and set aside.

In a medium bowl combine the pudding mix with the pineapple. Fold in the whipped topping.

Place one cake layer on a serving plate. Cover with one-third of the pineapple mixture and layer with one-third of the sliced strawberries. Repeat with the remaining two layers. Frost the side of the cake with the remaining pineapple mixture, if desired.

Refrigerate the cake overnight for the flavors to soak into the cake.

Makes 12 to 14 servings

Linda Denney, Queen
Crown Jewels,
Long Beach, Mississippi

Anna's Jam Cake

CAKE BATTER:
- 1/2 cup shortening
- 1 cup sugar
- 3 large egg yolks, well-beaten
- 1/2 cup blackberry jam
- 1 1/2 cups all-purpose flour
- 1/2 teaspoon salt
- 1 teaspoon cinnamon
- 1/2 cup buttermilk
- 3 large egg whites, beaten until stiff

FILLING:
- 1/4 cup blackberry jam
- 1/4 cup strawberry preserves
- 1/4 cup cherry preserves
- Chocolate syrup (optional)

Preheat the oven to 350 degrees. Line three 9-inch round baking pans with parchment paper. Set aside.

For the cake, in a large bowl cream the shortening and sugar with an electric mixer on medium-high speed. Add the egg yolks and the jam. Beat well.

In a medium bowl combine the flour, salt, and cinnamon. Add the dry ingredients to the creamed ingredients alternately with the buttermilk, beating well after each addition. Fold in the egg whites. Spoon the batter into the prepared pans. Bake 25 minutes. Cool on wire racks and remove from pans.

To assemble the cake, spread the blackberry jam on one layer. Top with the second layer and spread with the strawberry preserves. Add the third layer and spread with the cherry preserves. Drizzle with chocolate syrup, if desired, before serving.

Makes 12 to 15 servings

Betty Swift, Princess Lazy Bones
Purple Passion Flower Ladies,
Greensboro, North Carolina

Apricot Brandy Cake

1 cup (2 sticks) butter or margarine	1 teaspoon vanilla extract
3 cups granulated sugar	1 teaspoon orange extract
6 large eggs	1/2 teaspoon rum extract
3 cups all-purpose flour	1/2 teaspoon lemon extract
1/4 teaspoon baking soda	1/4 teaspoon almond extract
1/2 teaspoon salt	1/2 cup apricot brandy
1 cup sour cream	Confectioners' sugar, for garnish

Preheat the oven to 325 degrees. Grease and flour the bottom of a 10-inch tube pan. Set aside.

In a large bowl cream the butter and sugar. Add the eggs, one at a time, beating thoroughly after each addition. In a medium bowl combine the flour, baking soda, and salt. In a small bowl combine the sour cream, extracts, and brandy.

Add the flour mixture and the sour cream mixture to the sugar mixture. Mix just until blended with an electric mixture. Pour into the prepared pan.

Bake 70 to 80 minutes, or until a wooden pick inserted in the center comes out clean. Let cool in the pan on a wire rack. Remove the cake from the pan and sprinkle with confectioners' sugar.

Makes 20 servings

Ann Mandato, Princess of Pins and Needles
Chester Chicks,
Goshen, New York

Carrot Cake with a Twist

CAKE BATTER:

- 3 large eggs
- 1 cup vegetable oil
- 1/2 cup water
- 2 cups sugar
- 2 cups all-purpose flour
- 2 teaspoons baking soda
- 2 cups shredded carrots
- 1 cup chopped walnuts
- 1 (8-ounce) can crushed pineapple, drained
- 3/4 cup flaked sweetened coconut
- 1 1/2 teaspoons vanilla extract

ICING:

- 1 cup milk
- 1 (3.4-ounce) package instant French vanilla pudding
- 1 (8-ounce) container frozen whipped topping, thawed

Preheat the oven to 350 degrees. Grease and flour a 13 x 9-inch baking pan. Set aside.

For the cake, in a large bowl combine eggs, oil, water, and sugar. Mix until well combined. In a medium bowl combine the flour and baking soda. Stir into the egg mixture. Fold in the carrots, walnuts, pineapple, coconut, and vanilla, mixing well. Pour into the prepared pan. Bake 30 to 40 minutes, or until a wooden pick inserted in the center comes out clean. Let cool completely.

For the icing, in a medium bowl combine the milk and pudding, mixing well. Fold in the whipped topping. Spread on the cooled cake. Cover and refrigerate.

Makes 9 to 12 servings

Deborah Winters, Queen

Red Hat Pussycats,
Strasburg, Pennsylvania

Tangerine-Soaked Tea Cake

CAKE BATTER:

- 1/4 cup plain dry bread crumbs
  Zest from 3 tangerines or oranges
- 3 tablespoons tangerine or orange juice, preferably freshly squeezed
- 1 tablespoon freshly squeezed lemon juice
- 3 cups all-purpose flour
- 1/2 teaspoon baking soda
- 1/2 teaspoon salt
- 1 cup (2 sticks) unsalted butter, softened at room temperature
- 2 cups sugar
- 3 large eggs
- 1 cup buttermilk

GLAZE:

- 1/2 cup freshly squeezed tangerine juice
- 1 tablespoon freshly squeezed lemon juice
- 1/3 cup sugar

For the cake, preheat the oven to 350 degrees. Grease a 6-cup loaf pan. Line the bottom with parchment or waxed paper, pressing it in firmly. Pour the bread crumbs into the pan and shake to coat the sides, and then tip out any extra crumbs.

In a small bowl combine the tangerine zest, tangerine juice, and lemon juice. Stir and set aside.

In a medium bowl combine the flour, baking soda, and salt. Set aside.

In a mixer fitted with a paddle attachment or with a hand mixer, cream the butter until fluffy. Add the sugar and mix well. Add the eggs, one at a time, mixing well after each addition. With the mixer running at low speed, add the flour mixture alternately with the buttermilk until the batter is just mixed. Add the fruit juice and zest, mixing well.

Pour into the prepared pan and set the loaf pan on a baking sheet. Bake 70 to 80 minutes, or until the cake is firm in the center and a tester inserted into the center comes out dry and clean. Cool in the pan 15 minutes. Run a knife around the sides of the pan. Set a wire rack on a sheet pan with sides (to catch the glaze) and turn the cake out onto the rack. Remove the waxed paper.

For the glaze, in a bowl combine the tangerine juice, lemon juice, and sugar until the sugar is dissolved. Using a baster or pastry brush, spread the glaze over the top and sides of the cake and let soak in. Repeat until all the glaze has been used, including any glaze that has dripped onto the sheet pan. Let cool at room temperature or wrap in plastic wrap and store in the refrigerator for up to one week. Serve at room temperature, in thin slices.

Makes 12 to 15 servings

Linda Roberts, Web Site Mistress

Nonpareils Red Hat Club,
Knoxville, Tennessee

Whiskey Cake

CAKE BATTER:

- 1 (18.25-ounce) package golden butter cake mix
- 1 (3.4-ounce) package instant vanilla pudding
- 4 large eggs
- 1/2 cup rye whiskey
- 1/2 cup milk
- 1/2 cup vegetable oil
- 2 tablespoons sour cream
- 1/2 cup chopped walnuts
- 1/2 cup chocolate chips

GLAZE:

- 1/4 cup (1/2 stick) butter or margarine
- 1/4 cup rye whiskey
- 1/4 cup sugar

Preheat the oven to 350 degrees. Grease a 12-cup Bundt pan. Set aside.

For the cake, in a large bowl combine the cake mix, pudding mix, eggs, whiskey, milk, oil, and sour cream, beating well for 4 minutes on high speed with an electric mixer. Fold in the walnuts and chocolate chips. Pour into the prepared pan. Bake 45 to 50 minutes, or until a wooden pick inserted in the center comes out clean.

For the glaze, in a small saucepan cook the butter, whiskey, and sugar until the sugar has dissolved and the mixture is bubbly. Stir constantly. Pour the glaze over the top of the hot cake. Leave the cake in the pan for 2 hours. Remove from the pan and refrigerate.

Makes 12 to 14 servings

Pat Utterback, Princess Patrice

Siena Ya Ya Girls,
Las Vegas, Nevada

Lemon Cake

CAKE BATTER:

2   large eggs

1   (18.25-ounce) package lemon cake mix

1   (20-ounce) can lemon pie filling

ICING:

1   (8-ounce) package cream cheese, softened

1   tablespoon milk

1   teaspoon vanilla

4   cups confectioners' sugar

Preheat the oven to 325 degrees. Grease and flour a 13 x 9-inch baking pan. Set aside.

For the cake, in a large bowl combine the eggs, cake mix, and pie filling using an electric mixer. Mix until well blended. Spread into the prepared pan. Bake 30 to 35 minutes, or until a wooden pick inserted in the center comes out clean. Cool thoroughly.

For the icing, in a large bowl mix the cream cheese, milk, vanilla, and confectioners' sugar. Spread on the cooled cake.

Note: Lemon bars can be made using a 15 x 10-inch jelly-roll pan. Check doneness after 20 minutes.

Makes 12 to 15 servings

Marsha Konken, Lady Raspberry
Red Raspberry Tarts,
Sterling, Colorado

Lemon Pecan Fruitcake

1 (1-pound) package brown sugar	1/4 cup lemon extract
2 cups (4 sticks) butter	4 cups pecans, chopped
6 large eggs, separated and beaten	1/2 pound candied pineapple
4 cups all-purpose flour, divided	1/2 pound candied cherries
1 teaspoon baking powder	

In a large bowl cream together the brown sugar and butter. Add the beaten egg yolks, mixing well. Add 2 cups of the flour and the baking powder to the creamed mixture. Add the lemon extract.

In a medium bowl coat the pecans, pineapple, and cherries with the remaining 2 cups of flour. Add to the creamed mixture.

In a medium bowl beat the egg whites until stiff. Fold into the creamed mixture. Cover and let stand overnight in a cold oven.

The following day, preheat the oven to 250 degrees. Grease a 10-inch tube pan. Spoon the mixture into the prepared pan and bake 2 1/2 hours, or until a wooden pick inserted in the center comes out clean.

Makes 12 to 15 servings

Fredna McBride, Member

Scarlett Red Hatters,
Jacksonville, Florida

Chocolate Lover's Cake

This one went around the neighborhood when we were young marrieds. It has been a standby ever since.

1 (18.25-ounce) chocolate or chocolate fudge cake mix	1/2 cup water
1 (3.4-ounce) package instant chocolate pudding	4 large eggs
1 cup sour cream	1 (12-ounce) package chocolate chips
1/2 cup vegetable oil	Confectioners' sugar for dusting

Preheat the oven to 350 degrees. Grease and flour a 12-cup Bundt pan. Set aside.

Combine the cake mix, pudding mix, sour cream, oil, water, and eggs in a large bowl. Mix with an electric mixer on medium for 5 minutes. Fold in the chocolate chips. Pour the cake mixture into the prepared pan. Bake 50 to 55 minutes. Cool 5 minutes. Invert the pan and carefully remove the cake. Transfer to a serving plate and dust with confectioners' sugar. (Or drizzle with your favorite frosting.)

Makes 10 to 12 servings

Sue Ellen Cooper, Exalted Queen Mother

The Fabulous Founders,
Fullerton, California

Chocolate Lover's Fruitcake

This is a good "gifting" cake—unusual and delicious.

---

2   cups maraschino cherries, halved

2   cups chopped dates

2   cups pineapple tidbits, well drained

1   cup flaked coconut

2   cups walnuts, halved or chopped

2   cups pecan halves

2   (12-ounce) packages milk chocolate or semisweet chocolate chips

3/4 cup shortening

3/4 cup (11/2 sticks) butter

11/2 cups sugar

9   large eggs

3   cups all-purpose flour

1   tablespoon baking powder

1/2 teaspoon salt

1/2 cup unsweetened cocoa powder

2/3 cup crème de cacao

3   jiggers crème de cacao

Preheat the oven to 275 degrees. Grease three 9 x 5-inch loaf pans.

In a large bowl combine the cherries, dates, pineapple, coconut, walnuts, pecans, and chocolate chips. Mix gently but completely and set aside.

In a large bowl cream the shortening, butter, and sugar until fluffy. With the mixer on low, add the eggs, one at a time, beating well after each addition.

In a large bowl combine the flour, baking powder, salt, and cocoa powder. Slowly add the dry ingredients to the creamed ingredients. Beat on low for 30 seconds and then on high for 3 minutes. Add the fruit and nut mixture and 2/3 cup crème de cacao to the batter. Fold carefully until combined.

Spoon the batter into the prepared pans. Bake 2 to 2½ hours, or until a wooden pick inserted in the center comes out clean. (After 2 hours check every 15 minutes). Remove from the oven and cool thoroughly.

When cool, set each loaf on a large piece of plastic wrap and pour 1 jigger of creme de cacao over each loaf. Wrap tightly and put inside a ziptop plastic bag. Keep refrigerated for 3 to 4 weeks.

Makes 3 loaves (about 36 servings)

Sara Menke, Queen of Roses

Rosie Red Hats,
Wellington, Nevada

Chocolate Mocha Cake

A time-consuming recipe but well worth it for special occasions

CAKE BATTER:

1 cup unsweetened cocoa powder

2 cups hot strong coffee

1 cup (1/2 stick) unsalted butter, softened

2 1/2 cups sugar

4 large eggs, at room temperature

2 3/4 cups all-purpose flour

2 teaspoons baking soda

1/2 teaspoon baking powder

1/2 teaspoon salt

1 1/2 teaspoons vanilla extract

CREAM FILLING:

2 (3-ounce) packages cream cheese, softened

1/3 cup sugar

1 (8-ounce) container frozen whipped topping, thawed

CHOCOLATE ICING:

1 (6-ounce) package semisweet chocolate morsels

1/2 cup half-and-half

3/4 cup (1 1/2 sticks) butter or margarine

1/2 teaspoon instant coffee

2 1/2 cups sifted confectioners' sugar

Preheat the oven to 350 degrees. Line three 9-inch round cake pans with waxed paper. Grease and flour the waxed paper. Set aside.

For the cake, in a small bowl combine the cocoa powder and coffee, stirring until smooth. Set aside.

In a large bowl cream the butter. Gradually add the sugar, beating well at medium speed with an electric mixer. Add the eggs, one at a time, beating well after each addition.

In a medium bowl combine the flour, baking soda, baking powder, and salt. Add to the creamed mixture, alternately with cocoa mixture, beating at low speed of an electric mixer, beginning and ending with the flour mixture. Stir in the vanilla. Do not over beat. Pour the batter evenly into the prepared pans. Bake 20 to 25 minutes, or until a wooden pick inserted in the center comes out clean. Cool in the pans 10 minutes. Remove the cakes from the pans, peel off the waxed paper, and cool completely on wire racks.

For the cream filling, in a medium bowl beat together the cream cheese, sugar, and whipped topping. Place one layer of cake on a serving plate. Spread with half of the cream cheese mixture. Add the second layer and spread with the remaining cream cheese mixture. Top with the third layer.

For the icing, in a heavy saucepan, combine the chocolate morsels, half-and-half, butter, and instant coffee. Cook over medium heat, stirring until the chocolate melts. Remove from the heat. Stir in the confectioners' sugar, mixing well. Set the saucepan in a bowl of ice, and beat on low speed with an electric mixer until the icing holds its shape and loses its gloss. Add a few more drops of half-and-half if needed to make spreading consistency. Spread the icing on the top and side of cake. Refrigerate until ready to serve.

Makes 12 servings

Naomi Murray, Queen Mother
Scarlet O'Hatters of The Ozarks,
Springfield, Missouri

Mexican Chocolate Cake

CAKE BATTER:

- 1/2 cup (1 stick) margarine
- 1/2 cup vegetable oil
- 4 tablespoons unsweetened cocoa powder
- 1 cup water
- 2 cups all-purpose flour
- 1 teaspoon baking soda
- 2 cups sugar
- 1/2 cup sour milk*
- 2 large eggs, beaten
- 1 teaspoon cinnamon
- 1 teaspoon vanilla

ICING:

- 1/2 cup (1 stick) margarine
- 4 tablespoons unsweetened cocoa powder
- 6 tablespoons milk
- 1 (16-ounce) package confectioners' sugar
- 1 teaspoon vanilla extract
- 1/2 cup chopped pecans

Preheat the oven to 350 degrees. Grease an 18 x12-inch jelly-roll pan. Set aside

For the cake, in a medium saucepan combine the margarine, oil, cocoa powder, and water. Heat until the margarine is melted.

In a large bowl combine the flour, baking soda, and sugar.

In a medium bowl combine the sour milk, eggs, cinnamon, and vanilla. Blend with the flour mixture. Add the cocoa mixture, mixing well. Pour the batter into the prepared pan. Bake 20 to 25 minutes, or until a wooden pick inserted in the center comes out clean.

For the icing, in a medium saucepan combine the margarine, cocoa powder, and milk. Heat the mixture, stirring constantly, until bubbles form around the edge. Remove from the heat. Add the confectioners' sugar, vanilla, and pecans. Mix well and pour over the cake while still warm.

* To make sour milk pour 1 1/2 teaspoons vinegar in a measuring cup. Add enough milk to make 1/2 cup.

Makes 24 servings

Wanda Allison, Member
Houston Heights Red Hat Honeys,
Houston, Texas

International Red Hat Society Day, celebrated in Ottawa, Ontario, Canada. A pot luck dinner and card reading.

Back row L to R: *Arvilla Shouldice, Eleanor Anderson.*

Middle row L to R: *Tanya Vergette, Terry Durham, Georgie Charron.*

Front row L to R: *Jean Murphy , Sandy Nichol, Trudy Austin, Lynn Hill.*

Photo submitted by Arvilla Shouldice, Positively-Meno-Pausitive, Carleton Place, Ontario, Canada.

Chocolate Decadence Cake

1 (18.25-ounce) package chocolate cake mix	1/2 cup water
1 cup sour cream	1/2 cup miniature chocolate chips
1 (3.4-ounce) package chocolate instant pudding and pie filling	1 (8-square) package semisweet baking chocolate
4 large eggs	3 cups frozen whipped topping, thawed
1/2 cup vegetable oil	

Preheat the oven to 350 degrees. Lightly grease a 12-cup fluted tube pan or 10-inch tube pan. Set aside.

In a large bowl combine the cake mix, sour cream pudding mix, eggs, oil, and water. Mix on low speed with an electric mixer just until moistened. Beat on medium speed 2 minutes, scraping the bowl often. Stir in the chocolate chips and pour into the prepared pan. Bake 50 to 60 minutes, or until a toothpick inserted in the center comes out clean. Cool 10 minutes and then loosen the cake from the side of the pan with a knife and gently remove. Cool completely on a wire rack. Place on a serving plate.

In a microwave-safe bowl, combine the baking chocolate and whipped topping. Microwave on high 1 1/2 to 2 minutes, or until the chocolate is completely melted and the mixture is well blended, stirring after each minute. Drizzle over the cake. Store the cake in the refrigerator.

Makes 18 servings

Pat Foster, Queen
Dusty Desert Roses,
Desert Hot Springs, California

Fudge Rum Cake

CAKE BATTER:

- 1 (18.25-ounce) package fudge cake mix
- 1 (3.4-ounce) package vanilla instant pudding
- 1/2 cup rum
- 1/2 cup water
- 1/2 cup vegetable oil
- 4 large eggs

Sprinkle of cinnamon (to taste)
- 1/2 cup chopped pecans

GLAZE:

- 1 cup firmly packed dark brown sugar
- 1/2 cup (1 stick) butter
- 1/4 cup rum
- 1/4 cup water

Preheat the oven to 350 degrees. Grease and flour a 12-cup Bundt pan. Set aside.

For the cake, in a large bowl combine the cake mix, pudding mix, rum, water, oil, eggs, and cinnamon. Sprinkle the nuts in the bottom of the prepared pan. Pour the batter over it. Bake 50 to 60 minutes, or until a wooden pick inserted in the center comes out clean.

For the glaze, in a microwave-safe dish combine the brown sugar, butter, rum, and water. Cook in the microwave on high until boiling, stirring to dissolve the brown sugar. Carefully remove from the microwave and pour over the cake. Let stand 15 minutes before removing the cake from the pan.

Makes 12 to 15 servings

Sandy McConnell, Queen of Desserts
Dazzling Red Hat Sisters,
DeLand, Florida

Sweet Chocolate Muffin Cakes

2 cups (4 sticks) unsalted butter	8 large eggs
8 ounces sweet chocolate	2 teaspoons vanilla
3 1/2 cups sugar	4 cups coarsely chopped walnuts
2 cups all-purpose flour	36 walnut halves
1/8 teaspoon salt	

Preheat the oven to 300 degrees. Line 36 muffin tins with foil liners and coat with cooking spray. Set aside.

In the top of a double boiler melt the butter and chocolate over simmering water. Cool while mixing other ingredients.

In a large bowl combine the sugar, flour, and salt. Stir in the chocolate mixture. Whisk in the eggs and vanilla. Fold in the chopped walnuts.

Spoon the batter into the prepared muffin tins, filling about three-fourths full. Top each with a walnut half. Bake about 40 minutes, or until a wooden pick inserted in the center comes out clean. Cool on wire racks.

Makes 36 servings

Ellen Lathlean, Member

Crimson Tribe,
Pleasanton, California

Claire's Lavender and Lemon Cake

CAKE BATTER:

- 1 cup (2 sticks) butter, softened
- 1 (8-ounce) package cream cheese, softened
- 1 1/2 cups sugar
- 3 large eggs
- 1 1/2 teaspoons vanilla
- 2 tablespoons lemon juice

- 2 1/4 cups all-purpose flour, divided
- 1 1/2 teaspoons baking powder
- 1 tablespoon finely chopped lavender buds
- 1 tablespoon grated lemon zest

GLAZE:

- 1 cup confectioners' sugar
- 1/4 cup lemon juice

Preheat the oven to 350 degrees. Grease a 9-inch springform pan. Set aside.

For the cake, in a large bowl beat the butter and cream cheese until smooth. Add the sugar and eggs, one at a time, mixing well after each addition. Add the vanilla and lemon juice, mixing well. In a medium bowl combine 2 cups of the flour with the baking powder. Stir into the creamed batter.

In a small bowl combine the remaining 1/4 cup flour with the lavender and lemon zest. Stir into the batter. Pour the batter into the prepared pan. Bake 50 to 60 minutes, or until the cake is firm when gently pressed in the center. Cool on a wire rack for 5 minutes. Remove the cake from the pan and return to the rack to continue cooling.

For the glaze, combine the confectioners' sugar and lemon juice. Drizzle over the cake.

Makes 8 to 10 servings

Claire Knodell, Munkus the Brat

Red Hot Jazzy Ladies,
Kelowna, British Columbia

Spice Cake

CAKE BATTER:

2 cups firmly packed dark brown sugar

1/2 cup (1 stick) butter, softened

2 large eggs

21/2 cups all-purpose flour

11/2 teaspoons baking powder

1 teaspoon nutmeg

1 teaspoon allspice

1 teaspoon baking soda

2 teaspoons cinnamon

1 cup buttermilk

1 teaspoon vanilla

ICING:

1/2 cup (1 stick) butter

1 cup firmly packed dark brown sugar

1/4 cup milk

11/2 cups sifted confectioners' sugar

Preheat the oven to 350 degrees. Grease two 8-inch round cake pans or one 13 x 9-inch baking pan. Line the bottom of the pans with waxed paper and grease. Set aside.

For the cake, in a large bowl cream the sugar and butter together until fluffy. Add the eggs and beat just until mixed.

In a medium bowl combine the flour, baking powder, nutmeg, allspice, baking soda, and cinnamon. Add the dry ingredients alternately with the buttermilk to the creamed mixture, beating well after each addition. Stir in the vanilla. Pour into the prepared pan. Bake 30 to 35 minutes, or until a wooden pick inserted in the center comes out clean. Cool on wire racks before removing from the pan. Remove the waxed paper.

For the icing, in a medium saucepan melt the butter and stir in the brown sugar. Bring to a boil. Cook and stir over low heat for 2 minutes. Stir in the milk. Bring to a boil, stirring constantly. Remove from the heat and cool to lukewarm. Gradually beat in the confectioners' sugar. The icing should be thin. Frost the top and sides of the cake (and between layers if using 2 pans).

Makes 12 servings

Joanne Thill, Queen Mum
London Bridge Red Hots,
Lake Havasu City, Arizona

From L to R: *Doreen Carlson-Doyle, Deanne Deady, Linda Fleming, and Donna Rustand.*

Photo submitted by Doreen Carlson-Doyle, The Bend Red-Hot Bodacious Mountain Mommas, Bend, Oregon.

German Black Forest Cake

1 (21-ounce) can cherry pie filling
1 (8¹/2-ounce) can crushed pineapple, undrained
1 cup slivered almonds, toasted
1¹/2 cups semisweet chocolate morsels
1 cup flaked coconut

1 (18.25-ounce) package chocolate cake mix
¹/2 cup (1 stick) butter or margarine, melted
Whipped cream, for garnish

Preheat the oven to 350 degrees. Grease a 13 x 9-inch baking dish.

Pour the cherry pie filling into the prepared dish and spread evenly.

Spread the crushed pineapple over the cherry filling. Sprinkle with the almonds, chocolate morsels, and coconut. Sprinkle the cake mix over the top. Pour the melted butter evenly on top.

Cover with aluminum foil and bake 30 minutes. Remove the foil and bake 15 to 20 minutes longer, or until a wooden pick inserted in the center comes out clean. Serve with whipped cream.

Makes 10 to 12 servings

Linda Lee Parker, Royal Highness, Skye O'Malley
Roswell Red Hots,
Roswell, Georgia

Jewish Honey Cake

1¾ cups honey	3½ cups all-purpose flour
1 cup strong coffee	1 teaspoon baking soda
4 large eggs	2 teaspoons baking powder
2 tablespoons vegetable oil	1 teaspoon allspice
1 cup sugar	1 teaspoon cinnamon

Preheat the oven to 300 degrees. Grease two 9 x 5-inch loaf pans.

In a small saucepan bring the honey gently to a boil. Cool slightly and stir in the coffee. Set aside.

In a large bowl beat the eggs until light and lemon colored. Add the oil, gradually beating well to blend. Gradually beat in the sugar.

In a medium bowl combine the flour, baking soda, baking powder, allspice, and cinnamon. Add the dry ingredients to the creamed mixture alternately with the honey mixture, mixing well after each addition. Pour the batter into the prepared pans. Bake 1 hour, or until a wooden pick inserted in the center comes out clean. Cool and remove from the pans. Wrap well and store in a cool place. This cake keeps well.

Makes 16 to 20 servings

Elizabeth Wesley, Velvet Queen
Velvet Violettes,
Edmonton, Apounderta
Alberta, Canada

Mollie's Poppy Seed Chiffon Cake

1 cup (2 sticks) butter	1 cup sour cream
1½ cups sugar	1 tablespoon vanilla
4 large eggs, separated	2 ounces poppy seeds
1 teaspoon baking soda	Sifted confectioners' sugar, for garnish
2 cups all-purpose flour, sifted	

Preheat the oven to 350 degrees.

In a large bowl cream the butter and sugar. Stir in the egg yolks.

In a medium bowl combine the baking soda and flour. Add the flour mixture alternately with the sour cream to the creamed mixture. Stir in the vanilla.

In a medium bowl beat the egg whites until stiff. Gently fold into the batter. Spread the batter evenly in an ungreased 10-inch tube pan. Bake 1 hour.

Turn the pan upside down when done and cool thoroughly. Take a spatula and run it around the side of the pan. Remove the cake from the pan and place, rounded side up, on a serving plate. Sprinkle the cake with confectioners' sugar when the cake is totally cool.

Makes 10 to 12 servings

Stephanie Siebert, Lady Stephanie
Red Hat Rebels,
Las Vegas, Nevada

Award-Winning Red Velvet Cake

CAKE BATTER:

2 1/2 cups self-rising flour

1 1/2 cups sugar

2 large eggs

1 1/2 cups vegetable oil

1 tablespoon baking soda

1 tablespoon vanilla extract

1 ounce red food coloring

1 cup buttermilk

2 tablespoons unsweetened cocoa powder

1 tablespoon vinegar

ICING:

7 cups confectioners' sugar

2 (8-ounce) packages cream cheese, softened

3/4 cup (1 1/2 sticks) butter or margarine, softened

1 teaspoon vanilla

Preheat the oven to 350 degrees. Lightly grease and flour three 9-inch round cake pans.

For the cake, in a large bowl mix the flour, sugar, eggs, oil, baking soda, vanilla, and food coloring.

In a medium bowl combine the buttermilk, cocoa powder, and vinegar. Stir well. Pour into the flour mixture and blend well. Pour the batter into the prepared pans. Bake 15 to 20 minutes, or until the center springs back to the touch. Allow the cake to cool for 10 minutes and turn layers out onto waxed paper. Set aside to cool.

For the icing, in a large bowl whip together the confectioners' sugar, cream cheese, butter, and vanilla until creamy and thick. Place one cake layer on a plate and spread the top with icing. Repeat with the remaining two layers, spreading the icing over the top and side of the cake.

Makes 12 to 15 servings

Carlotta Wixon, Queen Mother

Sierra Sirens,
Grass Valley, California

Royal Swan Cake

CAKE BATTER:

2 1/4 cups cake flour

1 3/4 cups sugar

2 teaspoons baking powder

1/2 teaspoon salt

1/2 cup vegetable oil

7 large egg yolks

3/4 cup orange juice

2 teaspoons grated orange peel

2 1/2 teaspoons orange extract

1 teaspoon vanilla extract

10 large egg whites

1 teaspoon cream of tartar

ICING:

1 (8-ounce) package cream cheese, softened

2 tablespoons milk

1 cup (2 sticks) butter, softened

8 cups confectioners' sugar

2 tablespoons orange juice

1 tablespoon orange extract

Preheat the oven to 325 degrees. Grease three 9-inch cake pans and line with waxed paper.

For the cake, in a large bowl combine the cake flour, sugar, baking powder, and salt. Using an electric mixer, blend at low speed for 1 minute. Make a well in the dry ingredients, and add the oil, egg yolks, orange juice, orange peel, and extracts. Beat until smooth.

In another large mixing bowl combine the egg whites and cream of tartar. Beat until soft peaks form. Carefully fold the egg whites into the flour mixture. Pour the batter evenly into the prepared pans. Bake 25 to 30 minutes, or until a wooden pick inserted in the center comes out clean. Cool in the pans 10 minutes. Remove the cake from the pans and continue to cool on wire racks.

For the icing, in a large bowl combine the cream cheese, milk, butter, confectioners' sugar, orange juice, and orange extract. Beat until smooth and creamy. Spread the icing between the layers, on top, and on the side of the cake.

Makes 10 to 12 servings

Linda Pennington, Queen Bunny

Sassy Hattitudes,
Loganville, Georgia

Hatters' Dump-It Cake

---

1 (21-ounce) can crushed pineapple

1 (21-ounce) can cherry pie filling

1 (18.25-ounce) package yellow cake mix

1 cup (2 sticks) butter, cut into pats

Preheat the oven to 350 degrees. Combine the pineapple and cherry pie filling in a 13 x 9-inch baking dish and mix well. Sprinkle the cake mix on top and top with the butter. Do not mix! Bake 1 hour. Delicious served warm with ice cream.

Makes 12 to 15 servings

Joanne Augenstein, Queen of Mirth and Merriment

Red Birds of a Feather,
Yellow Springs, Ohio

Three-Day Coconut Cake

1 (16-ounce) container sour cream
1 (12-ounce) package frozen coconut
1 cup sugar
1 (18.25-ounce) package white cake mix
1 1/2 cups frozen whipped topping, thawed

In a small bowl blend the sour cream, frozen coconut, and sugar. Mix well, cover, and refrigerate overnight.

The following day, prepare the cake mix according to the package directions. Bake in two 8-inch round cake pans. Let cool completely. Using a long serrated knife, cut both layers in half horizontally. Set aside 1 cup of the coconut mixture. Place one cake layer on a cake plate and spread with one-third of the remaining coconut mixture. Top with the next layer and spread with the coconut mixture. Add the third layer and spread with the remaining coconut mixture. Top with the fourth cake layer.

In a medium bowl combine the reserved coconut mixture and the whipped topping. Frost the side and the top of the cake with the mixture. Cover and refrigerate for 3 days before eating.

Makes 15 to 18 servings

Barbara Rogers, Queen Mother
Glitter Girls,
Jane Lew,
West Virginia

Savory Cheesecakes and Pies

Creamy, fruity, and chocolaty staples on the dessert table

What are the first two words you think of when you hear the word "dessert"?

"Pie" and "cake," right? Deciding which came first is probably much like trying to solve which preceded the other—the chicken or the egg. And declaring which is better is like trying to decide whether dogs or cats make the best pets.

Let's call a truce. Pie—and the similar cheesecake—always show up at the top of any popularity list. The reason? Pie is just plain wonderful!

Butter Pecan Cheesecake

CRUST:

1¾ cups graham cracker crumbs

5 tablespoons sugar

1½ cups chopped pecans

6 tablespoons melted butter

FILLING:

3 (8-ounce) packages cream cheese, softened

1½ cups sugar

3 large eggs

2 cups sour cream

1½ teaspoons butter pecan extract

1¼ cups chopped pecans

SAUCE:

1¾ cups chopped pecans, toasted

1¼ cups butterscotch or caramel ice cream topping

2 cups whipped cream (optional)

Preheat the oven to 475 degrees. Cover the bottom of a 9-inch springform pan with aluminum foil, bringing it part way up the side to prevent drips.

For the crust, in a medium bowl combine the graham cracker crumbs, sugar, and pecans. Add the butter and stir well. Press the mixture into the bottom of the prepared pan, and set aside.

For the filling, in a large bowl cream together the cream cheese and sugar with an electric mixer. Add the eggs, one at a time, beating well after each addition. Add the butter pecan extract and pecans and stir well. Pour the filling over the crust. Bake 10 minutes. Reduce the temperature to 300 degrees. Bake an additional 50 minutes. Turn off the oven, open the door, and keep the cake in the oven for 1 hour. Remove the cake from the oven and allow it to cool at room temperature. Cover and refrigerate.

Before serving, remove the side of the springform pan. For the sauce, in a small bowl stir the toasted pecans into the butterscotch topping. Spoon the sauce over the cheesecake. Top with the whipped cream, if desired.

Makes 12 servings

Linda Brown, Member
Look! Purple Red Hatters,
Beavercreek, Ohio

Cherry Mandarin Cheese Pie

1   (8-ounce) package cream cheese, softened

1   (14-ounce) can sweetened condensed milk

1/3   cup reconstituted lemon juice

1   teaspoon vanilla extract

1   (9-inch) graham cracker piecrust

1   (20-ounce) can cherry pie filling, chilled

1   (8-ounce) can mandarin orange slices, drained

Beat the cream cheese until light and fluffy. Add condensed milk and blend. Stir in the lemon juice and vanilla. Pour into the piecrust. Chill 3 hours or until set.

Top with the cherry pie filling. Arrange the mandarin orange slices around the edge of the pie. Refrigerate until ready to serve.

Makes 6 to 8 servings

Judy Allread, Lady Roja
Vintage Vamps,
Novato, California

Mini Surprise Cheesecakes

CRUST:

1 1/2 cups chocolate graham cracker crumbs

4 tablespoons sugar

1/4 cup (1/2 stick) butter, melted

16 to 20 miniature peanut butter cups

FILLING:

2 (8-ounce) packages cream cheese, softened

1 cup sugar

1/4 cup all-purpose flour

1 teaspoon vanilla extract

2 large eggs

TOPPING:

1 1/2 cups sour cream

1/3 cup sugar

1/2 teaspoon vanilla extract

Dark chocolate shavings

Preheat the oven to 350 degrees. Place 16 to 20 paper cupcake liners in each cup of a standard muffin pan. Set aside.

For the crust, in a medium bowl combine the graham cracker crumbs, sugar, and melted butter, stirring until the crumbs are moistened. Press 1 tablespoon of the crumbs into the bottom of each cupcake liner. Place 1 peanut butter cup in the center of each crust.

For the filling, in a medium bowl beat the cream cheese with an electric mixer until fluffy. Add the sugar, flour, and vanilla, mixing well. Add the eggs, one at a time, beating well after each addition. Spoon the mixture over the peanut butter cups, filling three-fourths full. Bake 15 minutes, or until the cheesecakes are set.

While the cheesecakes are baking, prepare the topping. Mix the sour cream, sugar, and vanilla in a small bowl. Blend well. Carefully spread 1 tablespoon of the sour cream mixture over each cheesecake. Bake an additional 5 to 8 minutes, or until the topping is set. Cool completely. Refrigerate at least 1 hour or until serving time. Top with chocolate shavings.

Makes 16 to 20 servings

Loraine White, Queen High Roller

Dicey Dames,
Ormond Beach, Florida

From L to R: *Maureen Ryan and Miriam Nagle shaking it up.*

Photo submitted by JoAnn Porrello, Go for It Gals, Oakland Gardens, New York.

Frozen Orange Mini Cheesecakes

1 (8-ounce) container light spreadable cream cheese

1 (12-ounce) can thawed undiluted frozen orange juice concentrate, divided

1 tablespoon sugar

2 tablespoons grated orange rind

Chocolate sauce or raspberry purée

Grated orange rind, for garnish (optional)

In a large bowl combine the cream cheese with 8 ounces of the orange juice concentrate. Use the remainder for drinking or another use. Blend in the sugar and grated orange rind.

Line a muffin tin with 8 paper liners. Divide the filling evenly between the liners. Freeze for 2 hours or until firm. Before serving, remove the paper liners. Drizzle chocolate sauce or raspberry purée on a serving plate. Arrange the cheesecakes on the plate and garnish with grated orange rind, if desired.

Makes 8 servings

Carol Hummerstone, The Crown Royal

Jet Setters,
Cold Lake, Alberta, Canada

Royal No-Bake Chocolate Cheesecake

1½ cups semisweet chocolate chips

1 (8-ounce) plus 1 (3-ounce) packages cream cheese, softened

½ cup sugar

¼ cup (½ stick) butter, softened

2 cups frozen whipped topping, thawed

1 (8-inch) chocolate cookie piecrust

In a microwave-safe bowl melt the chocolate chips on High in the microwave 1½ to 2 minutes, or until smooth. Cool.

In a medium bowl beat the cream cheese, sugar, and butter together on medium speed with an electric mixer for 2 to 3 minutes.

Stir in the melted chocolate chips. Fold in the whipped topping. Spoon the mixture into the piecrust and refrigerate until ready to serve.

Makes 6 to 8 servings

Sharon Brown, Queen Mum

The Saintly Red Germain-iums,
St. Germain, Wisconsin

Pumpkin Cheesecake

CRUST:

- 6 tablespoons butter, softened
- 1 cup all-purpose flour
- 1/2 cup ground walnuts or pecans
- 2 tablespoons sugar

FILLING:

- 3 (8-ounce) packages cream cheese, softened
- 2 cups sugar
- 3 large eggs

- 1 (16-ounce) can pumpkin
- 1 teaspoon cinnamon
- 1/2 teaspoon ginger
- 1/4 teaspoon nutmeg

TOPPING:

- 1 (16-ounce) container sour cream
- 3 tablespoons sugar
- 1/2 cup ground walnuts or pecans (optional)

Preheat the oven to 375 degrees.

For the crust, in a food processor combine the butter, flour, nuts, and sugar. Pulse a few times until the mixture resembles course crumbs. Pat the mixture evenly into a 10-inch springform pan. Bake 18 to 20 minutes, or until golden brown. Cool.

For the filling, in a large bowl beat the cream cheese and sugar on medium speed with an electric mixer until smooth. Add the eggs, one at a time, beating after each addition. Add the pumpkin, cinnamon, ginger, and nutmeg. Scrape down the sides of bowl and beat until well combined. Pour into the cooled crust. Bake 50 to 60 minutes, or until the center is just set. Remove from the oven and increase the oven temperature to 500 degrees.

For the topping, in a small bowl combine the sour cream and sugar. Spoon the mixture evenly over the cheesecake. Bake 5 minutes. Cool. Sprinkle the nuts over the cake, if desired. Cover and refrigerate at least 4 hours or overnight. The cake may be made up to 2 days ahead of serving time.

Makes 12 to 16 servings

Barbara Weinberg, Princess of Past and Present

Dusty Desert Roses,
Cathedral City, California

Peanut Butter Pie

1	(8-ounce) package cream cheese, softened	1	(8-ounce) container frozen whipped topping, thawed
1/2	cup peanut butter (creamy or crunchy)	1	(9-inch) baked piecrust or graham cracker crust
1	cup confectioners' sugar		Chocolate syrup or chocolate chips, for garnish

In a large bowl combine the cream cheese, peanut butter, and confectioners' sugar, blending until well mixed. Fold in the whipped topping. Spoon the mixture into the prepared crust. Top with drizzled chocolate syrup or chocolate chips. Serve cold.

Makes 6 to 8 servings

Merna Price, Queen Mother

Thousand Island Belles,
Gananoque, Ontario, Canada

Fresh Blueberry Cream Pie

1/4 cup cold water	1/2 cup water
Pinch of salt	1 cup sugar
5 tablespoons all-purpose flour	1 (10-inch) piecrust, baked
1 quart fresh blueberries, washed and drained, divided	Whipped cream, for garnish

In a small bowl combine the cold water, salt, and flour. Mix into a paste and set aside.

In a medium saucepan combine 1 cup of the blueberries, the water, and sugar, cooking until the sugar dissolves. Remove from the heat and whisk in the flour mixture until smooth. Return to the heat and cook, stirring until the mixture is thickened. Remove the saucepan from the heat and cool. Stir in the remaining 3 cups blueberries. Pour into the piecrust and chill. Garnish with whipped cream before serving.

Makes 6 to 8 servings

Reyes Smith, Queen
Carefree Crimson Court of Coventry,
Royal Oak, Michigan

Mixed Berry Tartlets

Amazingly simple but delicious

3/4 cup (1 1/2 sticks) unsalted butter, cut into pieces

1/2 cup confectioners' sugar

1 1/2 cups all-purpose flour

1 1/2 cups heavy whipping cream

1 1/2 tablespoons sugar

3/4 teaspoon vanilla extract

8 tablespoons fruit preserves, any flavor

2 pints assorted fresh berries, tossed with a little sugar

With a mixer on low speed, beat the butter and confectioners' sugar until creamy. Gradually beat in the flour until the dough begins to come together. Gather the dough into a ball, divide into 8 pieces, and press into the bottom and up the sides of eight 4-inch tart pans with removable bottoms. Refrigerate for 15 minutes.

Preheat the oven to 350 degrees.

Arrange the tart pans on a cookie sheet and bake 14 to 16 minutes, or until just golden and baked through. Cool completely on a wire rack. Tap on the bottom of each pan to remove the crust.

In a medium bowl whip the cream, sugar, and vanilla until soft peaks form. Spread the bottom of each tartlet with 1 tablespoon of preserves. Spoon whipped cream over the preserves, filling to the top of each crust. Arrange the fruit on top. Keep refrigerated until ready to serve.

Makes 8 servings

Wanda Wendelken, Queen

Dixie Delights,
Arlington, Tennessee

Razzle Dazzle Berry Pie

1/2 cup sugar

3 tablespoons cornstarch

1/4 teaspoon salt

1/2 cup water

1 tablespoon fresh lemon juice

2 tablespoons butter or margarine

3 cups fresh sliced strawberries, blueberries, raspberries, or blackberries (or a combination)

2 cups whipping cream

2 tablespoons confectioners' sugar

1/2 teaspoon vanilla

1 (9-inch) piecrust, baked

In a medium saucepan combine the sugar, cornstarch, and salt. Stir in the water and lemon juice. Blend well. Cook on medium heat, whisking constantly, until the mixture boils and thickens. Remove from the heat. Stir in the butter and berries. Cool.

In a medium bowl whip the cream until stiff, blending in the confectioners' sugar and the vanilla. Spoon the berry mixture into the cooled crust. Top with the whipped cream and one perfect berry. Refrigerate at least 2 hours before serving.

Makes 6 to 8 servings

Joan Williams, Royal Member

Razzberry Tarts,
Belleair Beach, Florida

Strawberry Pie

6 cups fresh whole strawberries, divided

1 cup sugar

3 tablespoons cornstarch

1 tablespoon fresh lemon juice

1/4 teaspoon almond extract

1 (9-inch) piecrust or graham cracker crust, baked

Whipped cream, for garnish

In a medium saucepan mash 3 cups of the berries. Add the sugar and cornstarch, mixing well. Cook over medium-low heat, stirring constantly, for about 5 minutes or until thickened. Remove from the heat and cool 5 minutes. Add the remaining 3 cups of berries, the lemon juice, and almond extract. Pour into the prepared piecrust. Chill in the refrigerator about 4 hours. Before serving, top individual slices with whipped cream.

Makes 6 to 8 servings

Thelma Montecalvo,
Queen Supreme
Little Rhody Red Hens,
Woonsocket, Rhode Island

Orange Angel Pie

CRUST:

4 large egg whites
1/4 teaspoon cream of tartar
1 cup sugar
1/8 teaspoon salt

FILLING:

4 large egg yolks
1/2 cup sugar
Dash of salt

2 tablespoons orange juice
1 tablespoon lemon juice
1 teaspoon grated orange rind
1 teaspoon grated lemon rind

TOPPING:

1 cup whipping cream
2 tablespoons confectioners' sugar
Grated orange zest (optional)
Mandarin orange slices (optional)

Preheat the oven to 250 degrees.

For the crust, in a large bowl beat the egg whites until the foam is white. Beat in the cream of tartar. Add the sugar and salt. Continue beating until stiff peaks form. Press into a greased 9-inch pie pan, working around the edge like a piecrust, keeping it thinnest in the bottom. Bake 1 hour. Cool.

For the filling, in a medium bowl beat the egg yolks with the sugar and salt. Beat in the orange juice, lemon juice, orange rind, and lemon rind. Continue beating until well-blended. Place the mixture over hot water in a double boiler. Cook, stirring constantly, until thickened. Set aside.

For the topping, in a medium bowl whip the whipping cream until stiff. Fold in the confectioners' sugar. Spread half of the mixture over the cooled crust. Cover with the cooled filling. Spread the remaining whipped cream over the top. Chill for at least 12 hours.

To serve, top with grated orange zest and mandarin orange slices, if desired.

Makes 6 to 8 servings

Jane Taylor, Diva
Divas To Go,
Wooster, Ohio

Paradise Pineapple Pie

1 (14-ounce) can sweetened
   condensed milk

1 (8-ounce) container frozen
   whipped topping, thawed

1 (20-ounce) can crushed pineapple,
   well drained

1/3 cup lemon juice

2 (9-inch) graham cracker crusts

1/2 cup flaked coconut

In a large bowl blend the sweetened condensed milk, whipped topping, pineapple, and lemon juice with an electric mixer for 2 minutes until thickened. Pour the mixture evenly into the piecrusts. Sprinkle each pie with 1/4 cup coconut. Refrigerate until chilled before serving.

Makes 12 to 16 servings

Judy Roth, Queen Mum

*Rockin Red Hatters,
Warner, South Dakota*

Partridge in a Pear Tree Pie

3 cups fresh cranberries	1/4 teaspoon ground cinnamon
1 1/2 cups sugar	1/4 teaspoon salt
1 (8 1/4-ounce) can crushed pineapple	1 (8-ounce) can pear halves, drained and sliced in half lengthwise
2 unbaked (9-inch) piecrusts	Sugar (optional)
3 tablespoons all-purpose flour	

In a large saucepan combine the cranberries and sugar. Drain the pineapple, reserving 1/4 cup syrup. Add the syrup to the cranberries and cook over medium heat, stirring constantly, until the cranberries are tender, about 5 minutes. Cool.

Line one 9-inch pie plate with 1 of the piecrusts. Mix the flour, cinnamon, and salt in a small bowl. Stir into the cranberry mixture. Pour the cranberry mixture into the pastry-lined pie plate. Gently press the pear slices in a spoke-like fashion into the cranberry mixture.

Preheat the oven to 400 degrees. Roll out the remaining piecrust. Use a pastry knife to cut out small partridge, leaf, and pear shapes. Sprinkle with sugar, if desired. Place the shapes on an ungreased cookie sheet. Bake 7 to 8 minutes, or until golden. Bake the pie for 40 minutes. Arrange the cutouts on the baked pie.

Note: Fashion other pastry cutouts for a Christmas pie by using cookie cutters for bells, stars, and trees.

Makes 6 to 8 servings

Christine Austin, Princess Sunshine

Sassy Squaws of Seminole Lakes,
Punta Gorda, Florida

Amaretto Peach Tart

1 refrigerated (10-inch) piecrust	2 large eggs
1 (8-ounce) package cream cheese, softened	2 tablespoons peach preserves
1/3 cup sugar	2 cups fresh freestone peaches, sliced
3 tablespoons amaretto liqueur, divided	Whipped cream, for garnish

Preheat the oven to 450 degrees. Press the piecrust into a 10-inch tart pan with removable bottom. Generously prick the crust with a fork. Bake 7 to 9 minutes, or until light golden brown. Cool 30 minutes.

In a medium bowl combine the cream cheese, sugar, 2 tablespoons of the amaretto, and the eggs, blending well. Reduce the oven temperature to 375 degrees. Pour the cream cheese mixture into the cooled crust. Bake 15 to 18 minutes or until set. Cool 10 minutes. Refrigerate at least 1 hour.

Before serving combine the preserves and the remaining amaretto in a medium bowl. Arrange the sliced peaches on the filling. Pour the preserves topping over the peaches to coat. Garnish with whipped cream. Store any leftover tart in the refrigerator.

Note: To cover any cracks in the filling, dice additional peaches and cover the filling before adding the amaretto-coated peaches.

Makes 8 servings

Susie Van Foeken, Queen
Hilmar Red Hat Readers,
Hilmar, California

Queen Josephine's Muscadine Grape Pie

5 cups muscadine grapes, rinsed
1 cup sugar
1/4 cup all-purpose flour
1 tablespoon lemon juice
1 tablespoon lemon zest

1 (9-inch) deep dish piecrust
1 (9-inch) regular piecrust
2 tablespoons butter, cut into small pieces

Separate the pulp from the skins of the grapes. Set the skins aside.

In a large saucepan gently boil the pulp until the seeds loosen. Press the pulp through a sieve. Discard the seeds.

Cook the pulp and the skins until tender. Add water, if needed, to make 2 1/2 cups grape mixture.

Preheat the oven to 400 degrees.

In a small bowl combine the sugar and flour and add to the grape mixture. Add the lemon juice and lemon zest, mixing well. Cook on medium heat, stirring constantly, until thickened.

Pour the pie filling into the deep-dish piecrust. Top with the butter. Cover with the regular piecrust. Seal the edge and slit the top for steam to escape. Bake 40 minutes.

Makes 8 servings

Jo Ann Waterman, Queen Josephine
Elite Ladies of the Hat,
Franklinton, North Carolina

Raisin Pie

2 1/2 to 3 cups dark raisins
   Hot water
1 tablespoon lemon juice
3 medium egg yolks
1 cup whole buttermilk
1 tablespoon vinegar
3/4 cup sugar

2 tablespoons all-purpose flour
1/4 teaspoon salt
1 tablespoon grated orange rind
1 tablespoon grated lemon rind
2 unbaked (9-inch) piecrusts
1 large egg, beaten with a drop of water

In a medium saucepan combine the raisins with enough hot water to cover and the lemon juice. Cook over medium heat 5 minutes or until plumped.

In a large bowl beat the egg yolks. Add the buttermilk and vinegar, stirring to mix. Add the sugar, flour, salt, and grated rinds, mixing well. Drain the raisins and add to the mixture.

Preheat the oven to 450 degrees. Line a 9-inch pie plate with 1 of the piecrusts. Pour in the filling. Top with the remaining pastry, cutting a vent for steam to escape. Brush with the beaten egg.

Bake 10 minutes. Reduce the temperature to 350 degrees and continue baking 8 to 12 minutes, or until the crust is nicely browned. Remove from the oven. Serve while still warm or at room temperature.

Makes 8 servings

Sharon Sterbowicz, Queen
Red Hats in the Valley,
Huntingdon Valley, Pennsylvania

Grandma Ruby's Belgian Pies

PIE DOUGH:

2 ounces yeast compressed cake yeast

1/2 cup warm water

1/2 cup plus 1 tablespoon sugar, divided

6 large eggs

1 teaspoon salt

1 cup scalded cream

1 cup melted butter, cooled

5 cups all-purpose flour

  Belgian Pie Fillings

  Belgian Cheese Topping

In a small bowl dissolve the yeast in the warm water. Add 1 tablespoon of the sugar and let stand until it bubbles.

In a large bowl beat the eggs with the remaining 1/2 cup sugar and the salt. Add the scalded cream and melted butter. Add the yeast mixture to the eggs and blend in the flour slowly.

To knead the dough, flour your hands and use the heel of your hand to compress the dough and push away from you. Fold the dough back over itself until all the flour is folded in, being careful not to overknead, making the dough tough.

Cover the bowl with a dish towel, keep at room temperature, and allow the dough to rise until double in bulk (about 1 hour).

Divide the dough into 12 balls and press into twelve greased 9-inch pie pans. Let rise again to double in size.

Preheat the oven to 350 degrees. Cover each pie dough with one of the Belgian fruit fillings. (You will have 1 piecrust left for another pie of your choice.) Add the Belgian Cheese Topping over the fruit fillings. Bake 10 minutes on the lower oven rack and 5 minutes on the upper oven rack.

RAISIN FILLING (FOR THREE PIES)

1 (1-pound) package raisins
1 tablespoon cornstarch
1/3 cup sugar

In a medium saucepan combine the raisins with enough water to barely cover them. Cook 30 minutes, or until the raisins are tender. Mix the cornstarch with the sugar. Add to the raisins and water and simmer until thickened.

PRUNE FILLING (FOR FOUR PIES)

1 (1-pound) package pitted prunes
1/2 cup sugar

In a medium saucepan combine the prunes with enough water to barely cover them. Cook 1 hour, or until the prunes are tender. Drain, reserving the liquid. Use a food processor, blender, or grinder to mash the prunes. Add the sugar and enough reserved liquid to the ground prunes for a soft consistency.

APPLE FILLING (FOR FOUR PIES)

4 to 5 cups sliced pared baking apples
1/2 cup water
1 tablespoon cornstarch
1/2 cup sugar
1 (1-pound) package pitted prunes
1/2 cup sugar

In a medium saucepan cook the apples with the water about 20 minutes, or until the apples are soft. Combine the cornstarch and sugar in a small bowl. Add to the apple and water mixture. Simmer until thick.

(continued on the next page)

BELGIAN CHEESE TOPPING

1 (1-pound) container small-curd cottage cheese

1 (8-ounce) package cream cheese, softened

3 large egg yolks

1/2 cup sugar

1 teaspoon vanilla

In a large bowl combine the cottage cheese, cream cheese, egg yolks, sugar, and vanilla. Blend well.

This makes enough for 8 pie toppings. The remainder of the pies can be topped with whipped cream after baking and cooling.

Makes 12 pies of 6 to 8 servings each

Submitted by Jane Neverman,
Queen of the Internet,
for Arlene Jadin
Scarlet Divas of Dyckesville, Wisconsin

Chocolate Buttermilk Pie

1 1/2 cups semisweet chocolate chips
1 1/2 cups sugar
1/4 cup all-purpose flour
1/2 teaspoon salt
6 large eggs

1 cup buttermilk
1 1/2 tablespoons vanilla
1 (9-inch) frozen deep-dish piecrust, thawed
Whipped cream, for garnish

Preheat the oven to 325 degrees.

In a microwave-safe bowl, melt the chocolate chips in the microwave on high for 2 minutes, stirring every 30 seconds. In a medium bowl combine the sugar, flour, and salt, mixing well.

In a large bowl combine the eggs, buttermilk, and vanilla. Mix well with an electric mixer. Add the sugar mixture and mix well. Stir the melted chocolate into the batter. Pour the batter into the piecrust.

Bake on the middle rack in the oven for 1 hour and 15 minutes, or until the pie is crisp on top and a knife inserted in the center comes out clean. Remove from the oven and let the pie stand on a wire rack for at least 1 hour before serving. Garnish with whipped cream and serve warm or cool. Store leftover pie in the refrigerator.

Makes 8 servings

Margaret LeRoy, Queen Mother
Red Flamingos of Grandezza,
Estero, Florida

Blue Ribbon Creamy Apple Pie

1/2 cup (1 stick) plus 1 tablespoon margarine, divided

1/2 plus 2/3 cup sugar, divided

1 teaspoon vanilla, divided

1 cup all-purpose flour

1 (8-ounce) package light cream cheese, softened

1 large egg

4 cups thinly sliced McIntosh or Empire apples

1/2 teaspoon cinnamon

1/2 cup chopped pecans

Preheat the oven to 400 degrees.

In a large bowl combine 1/2 cup of the margarine, 1/4 cup of the sugar, and 1/2 teaspoon of the vanilla, beating well. Add the flour gradually, beating constantly until a soft dough is formed. Press the dough into the bottom and up the side of a 9-inch pie plate.

In a medium bowl combine the cream cheese, 1/4 cup of the sugar, egg, and remaining vanilla. Beat until smooth. Spread the mixture over the prepared pie shell.

In a medium bowl combine the apples, cinnamon, and the remaining sugar. Layer the apple mixture over the cream cheese mixture. Dot with the remaining margarine. Bake 15 minutes. Reduce the temperature to 350 degrees. Sprinkle the pecans on top of the pie. Bake 30 minutes, watching carefully so as not to burn the pecans. (Tent with aluminum foil, if necessary.) Serve warm or at room temperature.

Note: To make a lighter version, replace the sugar with Splenda.

Makes 6 to 8 servings

Mary Petruniak, Traveling Mary
Red Bonnet Sisters,
Lakeland, Florida

Chocolate Pie

2 cups plus 6 teaspoons sugar, divided

1/4 cup unsweetened cocoa powder

1/4 cup all-purpose flour

3 large eggs, separated

2 (12-ounce) cans evaporated milk

1/2 cup (1 stick) margarine

1 teaspoon vanilla

2 (9-inch) piecrusts, baked

In a large saucepan combine 2 cups of the sugar, the cocoa powder, flour, egg yolks, and evaporated milk. Cook over medium-high heat, stirring constantly, until thickened. Remove from the heat and stir in the margarine and vanilla. Blend well. Pour the mixture into the baked piecrusts.

In a large bowl beat the egg whites, gradually adding the remaining 6 teaspoons sugar. Beat until stiff peaks form. Spread on top of the pies. Place the pies under the broiler to lightly brown the meringue.

Makes 16 servings

Beverly Davis, Vice Queen Rambler
The Rambling Roses,
Villa Rica, Georgia

Coconut Custard Pie

1 (9-inch) piecrust	1/4 cup stick butter
1/2 cup plus 4 tablespoons sugar, divided	2 teaspoons vanilla, divided
1/3 cup all-purpose flour	6 ounces flaked coconut, divided
11/2 cups milk	1/4 teaspoon cream of tartar
4 large eggs, separated	1/8 teaspoon salt

Preheat the oven to 325 degrees. Bake the piecrust 8 to 10 minutes, or until lightly browned. Set aside to cool.

In a medium saucepan mix 1/2 cup of the sugar and the flour. Add the milk and stir until dissolved. Add the egg yolks and mix well. Cook the mixture over low heat, stirring constantly, until thickened. Remove from the heat and stir in the butter, 1 teaspoon of the vanilla, and 3 ounces of the coconut. Cool the mixture. Pour into the prepared piecrust.

In a large bowl beat the egg whites on high speed with an electric mixer until stiff but not dry. Sprinkle the cream of tartar and salt on top and beat slightly. Slowly add the remaining 4 tablespoons sugar and 1 teaspoon vanilla, beating constantly until the meringue forms soft peaks. Spread over the pie and sprinkle with the remaining 3 ounces of coconut. Bake 8 to 10 minutes, or until lightly browned. Remove from the oven and cool on a wire rack. Refrigerate leftovers.

Makes 8 servings

Charla Jordan, Queen of Quite a Lot
Brandon's Bodacious Babes,
Brandon, Mississippi

Honey Chocolate Pecan Pie

1   (9-inch) piecrust, unbaked
1/2 cup (1 stick) butter, melted
3/4 cup light corn syrup
1/4 cup honey
1   teaspoon vanilla

1/4 teaspoon salt
3   large eggs, beaten
1/4 cup shaved semisweet chocolate
1   cup pecan halves

Preheat the oven to 425 degrees. Press the piecrust into a pie pan and set aside.

In a large bowl combine the butter, corn syrup, honey, vanilla, and salt. Mix well, and then add the eggs, one at a time, beating well after each addition. Stir some of the chocolate into the filling and sprinkle a small amount over the crust. Arrange most of the pecan halves on the crust and cover with the filling. Top the pie with the remaining chocolate and the remaining pecans. Bake 10 minutes and then reduce the oven temperature to 325 degrees. Bake 40 minutes, or until the mixture is firm in the center. Cool on a wire rack.

Makes 8 servings

Linda Valentino, Queen Elegant Lady
Elegant Ladies in Red Hats,
Seminole, Florida

Lemon Chess Pie

2	large eggs	1	tablespoon yellow cornmeal
4	large egg yolks	1/4	cup lemon juice
1	cup sugar	1	tablespoon grated lemon rind
1/4	cup (1/2 stick) butter, melted	1	(9-inch) piecrust, unbaked
1/4	cup heavy cream		Whipped cream, for garnish
1	tablespoon all-purpose flour		Grated lemon rind, for garnish

Preheat the oven to 350 degrees.

In a large bowl beat the eggs, egg yolks, and sugar together at high speed with an electric mixer for 2 minutes. Add the butter and cream. Beat at high speed for 2 minutes longer. Add the flour, cornmeal, lemon juice, and lemon rind, mixing well. Pour the pie filling into the crust. Bake 45 to 60 minutes, or until a toothpick inserted in the center comes out clean and the top of the pie is medium brown. Cool to room temperature. Top with whipped cream and grated lemon rind before serving.

Makes 6 to 8 servings

Linda Roberts, Web Site Mistress

Nonpareils,
Knoxville, Tennessee

Sweet Potato Chiffon Pie

1 (0.25-ounce) envelope unflavored gelatin	2 large eggs, separated
3/4 cup sugar, divided	3/4 cup milk
1/2 teaspoon salt	1 cup mashed sweet potatoes
1/2 teaspoon cinnamon	1 cup whipped cream
1/2 teaspoon allspice	1 (10-inch) piecrust, baked
1/4 teaspoon ginger	Whipped cream, for garnish
1/4 teaspoon nutmeg	Toasted chopped pecans, for garnish

In a large saucepan combine the gelatin, 1/2 cup of the sugar, the salt, cinnamon, allspice, ginger, and nutmeg, stirring well. Beat the egg yolks slightly. Add the egg yolks, milk, and sweet potatoes to the saucepan. Cook over medium heat, stirring constantly, until the mixture boils and the gelatin dissolves. Remove from the heat and chill until partially set.

In a medium bowl beat the egg whites until soft peaks form. Gradually add the remaining 1/4 cup sugar and beat until stiff peaks form. Fold the beaten egg whites and the whipped cream into the sweet potato mixture. Spoon into the piecrust and chill until firm.

Serve with a dollop of whipped cream and toasted chopped pecans.

Makes 6 to 8 servings

Delilah Horsfield, Queen Mum
The Villages 1st Red Hatters,
The Villages, Florida

Pastry Delights

Specialties for breakfast or teatime—or anytime

When discussing pastries, the issue of when to eat them—before or after a meal—becomes moot. They do make great desserts, but serving them seems to be appropriate almost any time. Scones are good to have on hand as a delightful accompaniment to a spontaneous tea. Sticky buns can make breakfast special. Coffee cake or muffins can cozy up to a cup of coffee any time of day. Zucchini or banana bread make great accompaniments to an entrée. So, if you're looking for an excuse to bake, pastries provide a delicious one.

Sticky Buns

1/4 cup chopped pecans

1 (18 to 24-count) package frozen yeast dinner rolls

1 cup firmly packed light brown sugar

1/4 cup granulated sugar

1 (3.4-ounce) package butterscotch pudding (not instant)

1 teaspoon cinnamon

1/2 cup (1 stick) butter

Grease and flour a 12-cup Bundt pan. Place the pecans on the bottom of the pan.

Cut the frozen rolls into quarters. Place on top of the pecans. In a small bowl mix the sugars, pudding mix, and cinnamon. Cut in the butter and mix to make coarse crumbs. Sprinkle the mixture over the rolls.

Place the Bundt pan in a cold oven overnight. Do not cover. Rolls should rise overnight.

In the morning preheat the oven to 350 degrees. Bake the rolls 25 to 30 minutes. Invert the pan onto a plate and serve warm.

Makes 12 to 15 servings

Nancy Warrenfeltz, Red Writer

Pompous Sasses,
Pace, Fla

Almond Puffs

PASTRY:

1   cup (2 sticks) butter or margarine, divided

2   cups all-purpose flour, divided

1   cup plus 2 tablespoons water, divided

1   teaspoon almond extract

3   large eggs

ICING:

2   cups confectioners' sugar

1/4   cup (1/2 stick) butter, softened

1   teaspoon almond flavoring

3   tablespoons milk

Preheat the oven to 350 degrees.

For the pastry, in a large bowl cut 1/2 cup of the butter into 1 cup of the flour using a pastry cutter. Sprinkle 2 tablespoons of the water over the mixture. Mix well with a fork. Shape the dough into a ball. Divide the dough in half and pat each half into a strip, approximately 10 x 3 inches, on an ungreased baking sheet.

Heat the remaining butter and water. Bring to a rolling boil. Remove from heat and quickly stir in almond extract and remaining flour. Stir vigorously over low heat 1 minute, or until the mixture forms a ball. Remove from the heat. Add the eggs, beating until smooth. Spread the mixture evenly over the strips, covering completely. Bake 60 minutes, or until the topping is light brown. Set aside to cool.

For the icing, in a medium bowl mix the confectioners' sugar, butter, almond extract, and milk. Spread over the pastry. Cut into lady-like fingers to serve.

Makes 10 to 12 servings

Alice Bourque, Lady Alice
Flashy Floozies,
Salisbury, New Brunswick

Cake Mix Cinnamon Rolls

ROLLS:

  2 (0.25-ounce) packages dry yeast

2 1/2 cups warm water

  1 (18.25-ounce) package cake mix,
      any flavor

  5 cups all-purpose flour
      Softened butter or margarine
      Sugar and cinnamon
      Raisins (optional)

GLAZE:

1/2 cup confectioners' sugar

  1 teaspoon lemon juice

1/2 teaspoon vanilla extract

1/4 teaspoon almond extract

1/2 to 1 teaspoon water

For the rolls, in a large bowl combine the yeast and warm water. Let stand 5 minutes. Stir in the cake mix. Stir in the flour. Cover the bowl with a cloth and let the dough rise about 2 hours, or until doubled in bulk.

Roll out the dough onto a floured surface into a rectangle about 1/2 inch thick. Spread with softened butter. Cover evenly with sugar. Sprinkle with cinnamon according to your taste. Add raisins, if desired. Roll up the dough, starting from the long side. Chill 1 hour.

Preheat the oven to 350 degrees. Grease a 15 x10-inch jelly-roll pan.

Slice the chilled dough roll into 1/2-inch pieces. Place each slice on the prepared pan. Bake 25 minutes.

For the glaze, in a small bowl combine the confectioners' sugar, lemon juice, vanilla and almond extracts, and water. Mix well and pour over the warm rolls.

Makes 36 servings

Josephine Morrison, Queen Red Rover
Purple Playground Ladies,
Sand Springs, Oklahoma

Apple Dumplings

PASTRY:

2/3 cup lard or shortening

2 cups all-purpose flour

1 teaspoon salt

4 to 5 tablespoons cold water

FILLING:

6 medium apples, peeled and cored

3 tablespoons raisins

3 tablespoons chopped nuts

1/2 cup sugar

1/2 cup corn syrup

1 cup water

2 tablespoons butter

1/2 teaspoon ground cinnamon

Whipped cream (optional)

For the pastry, in a large bowl cut the lard into the flour and salt using a pastry cutter until the mixture is the size of coarse crumbs. Sprinkle with the cold water, 1 tablespoon at a time, tossing with a fork until all the flour is moistened and the pastry almost leaves the side of the bowl.

Gather the pastry into a ball. Roll two-thirds of the pastry into a 14-inch square. Cut into 4 squares. Roll the remaining pastry into a 14 x 7-inch rectangle. Cut into 2 squares.

Preheat the oven to 425 degrees. For the filling, place an apple on each square of pastry. In a small bowl mix the raisins and nuts. Fill each apple with the mixture. Moisten the corners of the pastry squares. Bring opposite corners up over each apple and pinch the edges of the pastry to seal.

Place the dumplings in an ungreased 13 x 9-inch baking dish. In a 2-quart saucepan heat the sugar, corn syrup, water, butter, and cinnamon. Bring to a boil, stirring occasionally. Boil 3 minutes. Carefully pour the syrup around the dumplings. Bake 40 minutes, or until the crust is golden and the apples are tender. Spoon the syrup over the dumplings two or three times during baking. Serve warm or cool with whipped cream, if desired.

Makes 6 servings

Karen Wolf, Empress of eBay
Delirious Redhatters,
Mount Gilead, Ohio

Auntie Joyce's Wine Biscuits

1	cup olive oil	2	tablespoons baking powder
1	cup sugar	4 1/2	cups all-purpose flour
1	cup port		Confectioners' sugar

Preheat the oven to 350 degrees.

In a large bowl combine the olive oil, sugar, port, and baking powder. Begin to add flour until you reach a soft, pliable consistency. Mix thoroughly (no kneading required). Flour a cutting board. Divide the dough into approximately equal portions, about a half-dollar in size. Roll each portion into a long pencil shape and twist into a knot. Place the biscuit knots on ungreased cookie sheets. Bake 20 minutes, or until light brown on top and dark on the bottom. Cool on wire racks. Sprinkle with confectioners' sugar, if desired.

Makes 90 biscuits

Joyce Torrice, Grandmama
Ruby Red Hat Ramblers,
Cranston, Rhode Island

Cranberry-Maple Nut Scones

SCONES:

2 1/2 cups baking mix

1/2 cup dried cranberries (or other dried fruit)

1/2 cup chopped walnuts

1/4 cup maple syrup

3 tablespoons firmly packed dark brown sugar

3 tablespoons milk

1 large egg

MAPLE GLAZE:

1/2 cup confectioners' sugar

2 teaspoons milk

1 teaspoon maple syrup

Preheat the oven to 425 degrees. Grease a cookie sheet. Set aside.

For the scones, in a medium bowl combine the baking mix, fruit, walnuts, syrup, brown sugar, milk, and egg, mixing until a soft dough forms. Turn the dough onto a surface dusted with baking mix or flour. Roll in the baking mix to coat. Shape into a ball. Knead the dough 10 times.

Pat the dough into an 8-inch circle and set on the prepared cookie sheet. (If the dough is sticky, coat fingers with baking mix.) Cut into 8 wedges but do not separate.

Bake 11 to 13 minutes, or until golden brown. Carefully separate the wedges.

For the glaze, in small bowl beat the confectioners' sugar, milk, and syrup until smooth. Drizzle the glaze over the scones. Serve warm.

Makes 8 servings

Toni Whitehead, Queen
Crawford County Cuties,
Van Buren, Arkansas

Currant Scones

2 cups all-purpose flour	3/4 cup milk
1/3 cup sugar	1 large egg
2 teaspoons baking powder	1/2 cup currants
1 teaspoon salt	1 large egg yolk
1/3 cup butter	2 tablespoons cold water

Preheat the oven to 350 degrees. Lightly coat a baking sheet with cooking spray. Set aside.

In a large bowl sift together the flour, sugar, baking powder, and salt. Cut the butter into the dry ingredients until the mixture is crumbly. In a small bowl beat together the milk and egg. Pour into the dry ingredients, stirring until well blended. Add the currants and mix well.

Prepare a flat surface by flouring it well. The dough will be slightly wet and will absorb the flour quickly. Place the dough on the surface and knead briefly. Pat the dough into a rectangle approximately 3/4 inch thick. Cut the scones with a 2 1/2-inch biscuit cutter and place on the prepared baking sheet.

In a small bowl beat the egg yolk with the cold water. Using a pastry brush, brush the egg wash over each scone. Bake 25 to 30 minutes, or until golden. Serve hot or cold with butter.

Makes 12 to 15 servings

Shery Goodman, Duchess of Gab

Frisky Foxy Females,
Sun City, Arizona

Grandma Sarah's Banana Bread

1 cup (2 sticks) margarine
2 cups sugar
4 large eggs, well beaten
2 teaspoons baking soda
1/4 teaspoon salt

2 1/2 cups all-purpose flour
6 ripe bananas, mashed
1 cup chopped walnuts or pecans (optional)

Preheat the oven to 350 degrees. Coat two 9 x 5-inch loaf pans with cooking spray. Set aside.

In a large bowl cream together the margarine and sugar. Add the eggs, baking soda, salt, and flour, mixing well. Add the bananas and nuts, if desired. Divide the batter among the loaf pans. Bake 50 minutes, or until a wooden pick inserted in the center comes out clean.

Makes 2 loaves

Stephanie Layer, Queen Cosmo
The Red Cosmopolitans,
Maplewood, Minnesota

Zucchini Bread

3 large eggs
1 cup vegetable oil
2 1/2 cups sugar
2 teaspoons vanilla
2 cups grated zucchini, well drained
3 cups all-purpose flour

1 teaspoon baking soda
1 teaspoon salt
1/4 teaspoon baking powder
2 teaspoons ground cinnamon
Chopped nuts, raisins, or chocolate chips (optional)

Preheat the oven to 350 degrees. Grease and flour two 9 x 5-inch loaf pans. Set aside.

In a large bowl beat the eggs, oil, sugar, and vanilla. Fold in the zucchini. Let stand 1 minute.

In a medium bowl combine the flour, baking soda, salt, baking powder, and cinnamon. Add to the zucchini mixture. Fold in nuts, raisins, or chocolate chips, if desired. Spoon the mixture evenly into the prepared loaf pans.

Bake 50 to 60 minutes, or until a wooden pick inserted in the center comes out clean.

Makes 2 loaves

M. Denise Chickey, Queen Denise
Kentucky Roses,
Erlanger, Kentucky

Sun Parlor Coffee Cake

Your guests will rave about this easy-to-make dessert.

1/2	cup firmly packed brown sugar	1	teaspoon vanilla
3/4	cup chopped nuts	1	cup sour cream
2	tablespoons cinnamon	1	teaspoon baking soda
1/2	cup (1 stick) butter	1 1/2	cups all-purpose flour
1	cup granulated sugar	1 1/2	teaspoons baking powder
2	large eggs		

Preheat the oven to 350 degrees. Grease a Bundt pan with cooking spray. Set aside.

In a medium bowl mix the brown sugar, nuts, and cinnamon. Sprinkle over the bottom of the prepared pan.

In a large bowl cream the butter and granulated sugar. Add the eggs and vanilla, mixing well. In a medium bowl combine the sour cream and baking soda. Mix gently and then add to the creamed mixture. Combine the flour and baking powder in a small bowl and then add to the creamed mixture. Drop by large spoonfuls into the prepared pan and smooth out the top. Bake 45 minutes. Remove from the oven. Cool on a wire rack for 15 minutes. Turn out on a serving plate. Serve warm or cool.

Makes 8 to 10 servings

Mary Jane MacVicar, Queen
Scarlett Shady Ladies,
Leamington, Ontario

Mom's Never-Fail Sour Cream Coffee Cake

1¼ cups sugar, divided
1 teaspoon cinnamon
½ cup (1 stick) butter or margarine
2 large eggs
1 cup sour cream
1 teaspoon baking soda

2 cups all-purpose flour
1 teaspoon vanilla
¾ cup chopped nuts (optional)
½ cup raisins, soaked in warm water until soft, then drained (optional)
½ cup chocolate chips (optional)

Preheat the oven to 350 degrees. Grease and flour a 9 x 5-inch loaf pan. Set aside.

In a small bowl mix ¼ cup of the sugar and the cinnamon. Set aside.

In a large bowl cream the butter and the remaining 1 cup sugar until well mixed. Add the eggs and blend well.

In a medium bowl mix the sour cream and baking soda. Add the sour cream mixture alternately with the flour to the egg mixture. Beat well after each addition. Stir in the vanilla. Pour half the batter into the prepared pan. Sprinkle with half of the sugar and cinnamon mixture. Top with nuts, raisins, or chocolate chips or all three, if desired. Add the remaining batter. Sprinkle with the remaining sugar and cinnamon mixture. Bake 1 hour. Cool in the pan on a wire rack for about 15 minutes. Remove the cake from the pan to a serving plate. Serve warm or cool.

Makes 8 servings

Stephanie Siebert, Lady Stephanie
Red Hat Rebels,
Las Vegas, Nevada

Dutch Apple Kuchen

2 tablespoons shortening
2 cups sugar
2 large eggs
2 cups all-purpose flour
2 teaspoons baking powder
  Pinch of salt
1 cup milk
4 cups sliced apples

TOPPING:
6 tablespoons sugar
4 teaspoons cinnamon
3 tablespoons melted butter

Preheat the oven to 350 degrees. Grease a 13 x 9-inch baking pan. Set aside.

In a large bowl cream the shortening, sugar, and eggs. In a medium bowl sift together the flour, baking powder, and salt. Add the flour mixture alternately with the milk into the creamed mixture, mixing well. Pour into the prepared pan. Top with the sliced apples.

For the topping, in a small bowl combine the sugar, cinnamon, and melted butter. Spread over the apples. Bake 30 minutes. Remove from the oven. Serve warm or cool.

Makes 15 servings

Yvonne LoCastro, Lady Potatia
Sophisticated Red Hat Ladies,
Auburn, New York

Oven-Baked Apple Pecan Brunch Cake

2 tart apples, peeled and sliced thin to equal 3 cups	1/2 cup milk
1/4 cup (1/2 stick) margarine	1/3 cup sugar, divided
1/4 cup chopped pecans	1 teaspoon cinnamon
3/4 cup pancake mix	Sour cream, for garnish
3 large eggs	Warm maple syrup, for garnish

Preheat the oven to 450 degrees. Grease a 9 x 9-inch baking dish. Set aside.

In a medium skillet sauté the apples in the margarine until tender. Pour into the prepared baking dish. Sprinkle the pecans over the apples.

In a medium bowl combine the pancake mix, eggs, milk, and 1 teaspoon of the sugar, mixing well. Pour evenly over the apple mixture. Mix the remaining sugar with the cinnamon and sprinkle on top. Cover tightly with aluminum foil and bake 10 to 12 minutes, or until the batter is puffed and the sugar is melted. Serve with sour cream and warm maple syrup.

Makes 4 to 6 servings

Josephine Morrison, Queen Red Rover
Purple Playground Ladies,
Sand Springs, Oklahoma

Orange Strawberry Eclairs

SHELLS:

1/2 cup (1 stick) butter

1 cup water

1/4 teaspoon salt

1 cup all-purpose flour

4 large eggs

ORANGE CREAM FILLING:

3/4 cup sugar

1/4 cup all-purpose flour

1/4 teaspoon salt

11/4 cups milk

6 large egg yolks

1/4 cup orange liqueur

11/2 cups heavy cream

CHOCOLATE GLAZE:

2 ounces bittersweet chocolate

2 tablespoons butter

1 cup confectioners' sugar

3 tablespoons milk

Fresh strawberries, sliced, or fresh red raspberries

Preheat the oven to 375 degrees. Grease a large cookie sheet or use a nonstick baking sheet. Set aside.

For the shells, in 2-quart saucepan, heat the butter, water, and salt, stirring until the butter melts and the mixture boils. Remove from the heat. Vigorously stir in the flour with a wooden spoon until the mixture forms a ball and leaves the side of the pan. Stir in the eggs, one at a time, beating well after each addition. Spoon the mixture into a pastry bag fitted with a very large plain tube. Pipe the mixture onto the prepared cookie sheet into twelve 4 x 1-inch strips (or twenty-four 2-inch mounds). Round the ends slightly. Bake 40 minutes, or until lightly browned. With the tip of a paring knife, cut a small slit on both sides of each shell to let the steam escape. Bake 10 minutes longer. Cool on wire racks.

For the filling, mix the sugar, flour, and salt in a 2-quart saucepan. Stir in the milk. Cook over medium heat. Bring to a boil, stirring constantly. Boil for 1 minute.

In a small bowl beat the egg yolks slightly with a fork. Beat a small amount of the hot milk mixture into the yolks. Slowly pour the yolk mixture back into the milk. Cook, stirring constantly, until the mixture thickens and coats the back of a spoon, about 8 minutes. Do not boil. Remove from the heat. Stir in the orange liqueur. Cover the custard surface with plastic wrap. Chill for about 2 hours. Beat the heavy cream until stiff peaks form. Fold into the custard.

For the glaze, in 1-quart saucepan melt the chocolate and butter over low heat, stirring constantly. Add the confectioners' sugar and milk, stirring until smooth. Let stand to thicken.

Slice each shell in half horizontally. Remove any dough from the center of the shells. Fill the bottom of the shells with the filling. Top with the berries. Replace the tops. Spread with the glaze. Refrigerate until serving time but not too long or the shells will get soggy.

Makes 8 to 12 servings

Sally Cecil, Countess of Cuisine

Scarlet Brims of Canonsburg,
Pittsburgh, Pennsylvania

Austrian Nut Horns

FILLING:

- 2 large egg whites
- 1 cup finely chopped walnuts
- 6 soda crackers, crumbled into small pieces
- 1/2 cup sugar
- 1 teaspoon vanilla

DOUGH:

- 2 cups all-purpose flour
- 1 (0.6-ounce) compressed yeast cake, crumbled
- 1/2 cup (1 stick) butter
- 2 large egg yolks
- 1/2 cup sour cream
- 1/2 cup sugar
- 1 large egg, beaten
- Sugar (optional)

For the filling, in a medium bowl beat the egg whites until stiff peaks form. In a small bowl combine the walnuts, cracker crumbs, sugar, and vanilla. Fold into the egg whites.

For the dough, in a large bowl combine the flour and yeast. Using a pastry blender, cut in the butter. Add the egg yolks and sour cream, mixing well. Knead for 5 to 10 minutes to smooth the dough. Refrigerate for 1 hour.

Preheat the oven to 375 degrees. Grease a cookie sheet.

Roll out the dough, 1 teaspoon at a time, in the sugar. Spread with 1/2 teaspoon of the filling. Roll up like a jellyroll, shape into horns, and place on the prepared cookie sheet. Brush with beaten egg wash. Bake 20 to 25 minutes. Sprinkle with sugar, if desired.

Makes 4 dozen

Elaine Strong, Queen Elaine
Diamond Divas of Sonora,
Sahuarita, Arizona

Rhubarb Muffins

1 1/2 cups granulated sugar
2/3 cup vegetable oil
1 cup buttermilk
1 large egg, beaten
1 teaspoon vanilla
1 teaspoon baking soda

1/2 teaspoon salt
2 2/3 cups all-purpose flour
2 cups diced rhubarb
1 cup chopped pecans
1 teaspoon cinnamon
1 teaspoon brown sugar

Preheat the oven to 350 degrees. Grease a muffin tin or line with paper liners. Set aside.

In a large bowl cream the granulated sugar, oil, buttermilk, egg, and vanilla. Add the baking soda, salt, and flour. Mix well. Fold in the rhubarb and pecans. Spoon the mixture into the prepared muffin pan. In a small bowl combine the cinnamon and brown sugar. Sprinkle over the muffins. Bake 25 to 30 minutes, or until a wooden pick inserted in the center comes out clean.

Makes 12 muffins

Stephanie Layer, Queen Cosmo
The Red Cosmopolitan's,
Maplewood, Minnesota

Strawberry Orange Muffins

1¼ cups halved strawberries

3 teaspoons butter, softened

2 teaspoons grated orange rind

2 large eggs

1½ cups all-purpose flour

1¼ cups plus 2 teaspoons sugar, divided

1 teaspoon baking powder

1/2 teaspoon salt

Preheat oven to 400 degrees. Coat a muffin tin with cooking spray. Set aside.

Combine the strawberries, butter, orange rind, and eggs in a blender. Process just until mixed.

In a large bowl combine the flour, 1¼ cups of the sugar, the baking powder, and salt. Add the strawberry mixture to the flour mixture, stirring just until moist. Spoon the batter into the prepared muffin tin. Sprinkle with the remaining 2 teaspoons sugar. Bake 20 minutes, or until the muffins spring back when touched lightly in center. Remove from the pan immediately.

Makes 12 muffins

Barbara Sierra-Franco, Princess of Prussia

Purple Queens of Prussia,
King of Prussia, Pennsylvania

Red Hat Blueberry Napoleons

1/2	package frozen puffed pastry sheets, thawed
1/2	cup sugar
2	tablespoons cornstarch
1/8	teaspoon salt
1/2	cup evaporated milk
1/2	cup water
1	cup half-and-half
3	large egg yolks, lightly beaten
1	teaspoon vanilla extract
1	teaspoon butter

BLUEBERRY FILLING:

1	(12-ounce) package frozen blueberries, divided
3/4	cup water
2	tablespoons cornstarch
1/2	cup sugar
1	teaspoon lemon juice
	Whipped cream
6	maraschino cherries

Unroll the puffed pastry, cut into 6 equal pieces, and place on a baking sheet 1 to 2 inches apart. Bake according to the package directions and cool thoroughly.

In a medium saucepan mix the salt, sugar, and cornstarch. Blend in the milk, water, and half-and-half. Cook over medium heat, stirring constantly. When mixture starts to thicken, add egg yolks. Continue cooking until mixture is bubbly and slightly thickened. (It will thicken more as it cools so don't overcook.) Remove from the heat and add vanilla and butter. Pour into a bowl and cover with plastic wrap, making sure the plastic touches the top of the custard. Cool completely in the refrigerator.

For the filling, in a medium saucepan cook half of the blueberries and the water over medium heat for 2 to 3 minutes. In a small bowl combine the cornstarch, sugar, lemon juice, and the remaining berries. Stir into the saucepan and continue cooking until the mixture turns clear and thickens. Cool completely.

To serve, slice the rectangles in half horizontally with a sharp knife. Arrange the bottom half on a dessert plate. Spoon 2 or 3 tablespoons of custard onto each pastry bottom. Top with 2 tablespoons filling, allowing the filling to run over the sides and onto the plate. Add a large spoonful of whipped cream. Top with the other half of the puffed pastry, more whipped cream, and a cherry.

Makes 6 servings

Rosa West, Queen Birdie

Red Hat Seagalls,
Piedmont, South Carolina

Florida-Style Beignets

1	cup water	1	teaspoon salt
1	cup whole milk	2	teaspoons sugar
1	medium egg		Pinch of nutmeg
3	cups all-purpose flour		Vegetable oil for frying
2	tablespoons baking powder		Confectioners' sugar, for garnish

In a large bowl mix the water, milk, and egg. Slowly add the flour, baking powder, salt, and sugar. Mix well. Add the nutmeg, mixing well.

In a Dutch oven heat 3 inches of vegetable oil over medium-high heat until hot. Drop the batter by spoonfuls into the oil. Fry, turning 2 or 3 times, until golden brown. Drain on paper towels. Dredge in the confectioners' sugar. Serve warm.

Makes 1 1/2 dozen beignets

Mary Chiocchi, Past Queen

Red Hat Rebels,
Port Charlotte, Florida

Easy Fruit Strudels

1 cup sour cream
1 cup (2 sticks) butter or margarine, softened
2 cups all-purpose flour
1 (18-ounce) jar pineapple preserves

1 (18-ounce) jar strawberry preserves
Coconut, raisins, and chopped nuts
Confectioners' sugar, for garnish

In a medium bowl mix the sour cream, butter, and flour. Blend well. Chill overnight.

Preheat the oven to 350 degrees. Grease 2 cookie sheets. Set aside.

Divide the chilled dough into 4 equal parts. Roll out one dough portion very thin on a floured pastry cloth. (Keep the dough that is not being rolled in the refrigerator.) Spread a small amount of both preserves on the dough. Do not spread too much or get too close to the edges of the dough. Sprinkle with coconut, raisins, and nuts. Fold in each short end and roll the dough tightly. Make sure the seam is on the bottom. Repeat the process with the 3 remaining dough pieces. Bake on the prepared cookie sheet 40 minutes. Remove from the oven and slice immediately. Sprinkle with confectioners' sugar when cool.

Makes 4 strudels, about 25 to 30 servings

Patsy Goodman, Queen Tat Pat
Red Hat Lacers,
Chula Vista, California

Munchable Cookies

No empty cookie jar with these choices

Cookies are probably the first dessert children learn about. The family cookie jar on the usually hard-to-reach countertop is the Holy Grail of toddler-kind. It represents all that is wonderful, yet hard to obtain. If not for cookie jars, a lot of cartoonists would have found themselves "reaching" for material. We can be thankful that cookies of all shapes and flavors (and jars to put them in) are a staple of modern life!

Cranberry Pecan Sandies

1 (15.6-ounce) package cranberry quick bread mix	1 tablespoon plus 4 teaspoons orange juice, divided
1/2 cup (1 stick) butter, melted	3/4 cup chopped pecans
1 large egg	30 to 36 pecan halves
	1 cup confectioners' sugar

Preheat the oven to 350 degrees.

In a large bowl combine the bread mix, butter, egg, and 1 tablespoon of the orange juice. Stir in the chopped pecans. Roll the dough into 1-inch balls. Place 2 inches apart on ungreased baking sheets. Press a pecan half into the center of each cookie. Bake 12 to 14 minutes, or until lightly browned. Cool 1 minute before removing to wire racks.

In a small bowl whisk the confectioners' sugar and the remaining 4 teaspoons orange juice. Drizzle over the cookies.

Makes 3 dozen cookies

Sheila Bougher, Queenie
Holy Rollers,
Owasso, Oklahoma

Sugar Cookies

1 cup sugar	1 1/2 cups all-purpose flour
Pinch of salt	1 1/2 teaspoons baking powder
1/2 cup (1 stick) butter, melted	1/2 teaspoon baking soda
1 large egg	Dash of nutmeg
1 teaspoon vanilla extract	

Preheat the oven to 350 degrees.

In a large bowl mix the sugar, salt, melted butter, egg, and vanilla. Sift in the flour, baking powder, baking soda, and nutmeg. Mix well. Roll the dough into small balls and place on an ungreased cookie sheet. Press with a fork to flatten. Bake 10 to 12 minutes, or until cookies are brown around the edges. Place on brown paper to cool. Store in an airtight cookie tin.

Makes 5 dozen cookies

Delilah Horsfield, Queen Mum
The Villages 1st Red Hatters,
The Villages, Florida

Chocolate Macaroons

2 cups firmly packed dark brown sugar

1/2 cup whole milk

1/2 cup shortening

1/2 teaspoon salt

6 tablespoons unsweetened cocoa powder

2 cups oatmeal

1 cup flaked coconut

1/2 cup chopped pecans or walnuts (optional)

In a large saucepan combine the brown sugar, milk, shortening, and salt. Bring to a boil over high heat. Boil 5 minutes. Remove the pan from the heat and let cool slightly. Add the cocoa powder, oatmeal, coconut, and nuts, if desired. Drop the batter by teaspoonsful onto waxed paper. Let stand until firm. Store in a covered container.

Makes about 30 cookies

Lois Pare, Queen Silly Bear
BEARy Hot Hatters,
Granby, Massachusetts

Chocolate Banana Chocolate Chip Cookies

1¼ cups all-purpose flour

¾ cup whole-wheat flour

⅓ cup unsweetened cocoa powder

1 teaspoon baking powder

½ teaspoon cinnamon

¼ teaspoon salt

1 cup firmly packed light brown sugar

¼ cup granulated sugar

½ cup (1 stick) butter or margarine, softened

2 large eggs

1 teaspoon pure vanilla extract

3 small extra-ripe bananas, thoroughly mashed

1 cup semisweet chocolate chips

1 cup chopped walnuts

Preheat the oven to 350 degrees. Grease a cookie sheet. Set aside.

In a large bowl combine the flours, cocoa powder, baking powder, cinnamon, and salt.

In another bowl combine the sugars and butter and beat until fluffy. Add the eggs, vanilla, and bananas. Add the sugar mixture to the flour mixture and beat until smooth. Stir in the chocolate chips and walnuts. Drop by tablespoonsful, 2 inches apart, onto the prepared cookie sheet. Add a little flour if batter is runny.

Bake 15 minutes. Let cool on the pan for about 2 minutes. Remove to a cooling rack. Store tightly covered. These also freeze well.

Makes 3 dozen cookies

Joanne Harter, Lady HiJinks, Court Jester

Hot Tamales of Watertown,
Harrisville, New York

Chocolate Chips Cookies Plus

1/3 cup shortening	1/2 teaspoon baking soda
1/3 cup butter, softened	1/2 teaspoon salt
1/2 cup granulated sugar	1/2 cup chunky or smooth peanut butter
1/2 cup firmly packed brown sugar	
1 large egg	1 (6-ounce) package semisweet chocolate chips
1 teaspoon vanilla	
1 1/2 cups all-purpose flour	1/2 cup chopped peanuts (optional)

Preheat the oven to 375 degrees.

In a large bowl cream the shortening, butter, sugars, egg, and vanilla.

In a medium bowl sift together the flour, baking soda, and salt. Set aside one-third of the mixture and stir the remaining two-thirds into the creamed mixture. Add the peanut butter to the creamed mixture. Coat the chocolate chips with the reserved flour mixture and add to the batter. Add the peanuts, if desired.

Drop the dough by rounded teaspoons about 2 inches apart on a baking sheet. Bake 8 to 10 minutes, or until delicately browned (cookies should still be soft). Cool slightly before removing from baking sheet.

Note: For a softer, more rounded cookie use 1 3/4 cups flour.

Makes 2 dozen cookies

Lois A. Garfield, Queen Mum
Jen Jo's Crown Jewels,
San Diego, California

Anise Italian Cookies

1 cup (2 sticks) margarine, softened	1 (2-ounce) bottle anise or lemon extract
¾ cup sugar	1 cup confectioners' sugar
3 cups all-purpose flour	Small amount of half-and-half
3 teaspoons baking powder	Few drops of vanilla extract
3 large eggs, lightly beaten	

Preheat the oven to 350 degrees.

In a large bowl cream together the margarine and sugar. Add the flour and baking powder and mix until crumbly. Add the eggs. Stir in the anise or lemon extract. Mix well. Drop the dough by teaspoonsful onto an ungreased cookie sheet. Bake 15 minutes, or until golden brown.

In a small bowl combine the confectioners' sugar with the half-and-half and vanilla. (The mixture should be thin but not runny.) Brush the warm cookies with the topping.

Makes 3 dozen cookies

Dolores Russo, Queen Dee Dee

Salty Belles of Winthrop,
Winthrop, Massachusetts

Bon Bon Cookies

1/2 cup (1 stick) butter, softened

13/4 cups sifted confectioners' sugar, divided

2 tablespoons vanilla, divided

11/2 cups all-purpose flour

1/8 teaspoon salt

Cherries, dates, nuts, or chocolate pieces for filling

2 tablespoons cream

Few drops of food coloring

Colored sugar, jimmies, coconut (optional)

Preheat the oven to 350 degrees.

In a large bowl combine the butter, 3/4 cup of the confectioners' sugar, and 1 tablespoon of the vanilla, mixing well. Blend in the flour and salt. If the dough is dry, add 1 to 2 tablespoons cream. Wrap 1 tablespoon of dough around a cherry, date, nuts, or chocolate pieces. Place the dough balls 1 inch apart on an ungreased baking sheet. Bake 10 to 12 minutes, or until set but not brown. Cool.

In a small bowl combine the remaining 1 cup confectioners' sugar, the cream, the remaining 1 tablespoon vanilla, and the food coloring. Dip the tops of the cookies in the icing. Set on wire racks for the icing to set. Top the cookies with colored sugar, jimmies, or coconut, if desired.

Makes 2 dozen cookies

Dolores, Fiori, Queen of Tea-light

Tea-lightful Red Hatters,
Hammonton, New Jersey

Nut Kisses

2 large egg whites	1/8 teaspoon salt
1/2 cup sugar	1/2 cup finely chopped pecans
1/2 teaspoon vanilla	

Preheat the oven to 275 degrees. In a large bowl beat the egg whites until stiff peaks form. Add the sugar a little at a time until all used. Fold in the vanilla, salt, and pecans. Drop the batter by teaspoonsful onto ungreased cookie sheets. Bake 50 to 60 minutes, or until the cookies feel dry. Cool slightly before removing from the pan.

Makes 2 dozen cookies

Linda Quinn, Sassie Lassie
Red Hat Tamales,
Bartlesville, Oklahoma

From L to R: *Marie Eves and Faith Eaton showing their fruit cups.*

Photo submitted by Faith Eaton, Jamaica Bay YaYa's, Ft. Myer's, Florida.

Carrot Walnut Cookies

1/2 cup (1 stick) butter, softened

1 1/4 cups firmly packed light brown sugar

2 (4-ounce) jars baby food carrots

1 large egg

1 tablespoon freshly grated orange peel

1/2 cup fresh orange juice

1 teaspoon baking soda

1 teaspoon ground cinnamon

1/2 teaspoon salt

1/2 teaspoon ground nutmeg

1/3 teaspoon ground cloves

2 1/2 cups all-purpose flour

1 cup chopped walnuts

ORANGE CREAM CHEESE ICING:

1 (3-ounce) package 1/3 less-fat cream cheese, softened

2 tablespoons butter, softened

1 teaspoon freshly grated orange peel

2 tablespoons fresh orange juice

2 1/2 cups confectioners' sugar

1/2 cup chopped walnuts

Preheat the oven to 350 degrees.

In a large bowl beat the butter and brown sugar with an electric mixer on medium speed until creamy. Beat in the carrots, egg, orange peel, orange juice, baking soda, cinnamon, salt, nutmeg, and cloves until blended. (The mixture may look curdled.) With mixer on low speed, beat in the flour just until blended. Stir in the walnuts. Drop by rounded teaspoonsful 2 inches apart on an ungreased baking sheet. Bake 10 to 12 minutes, or until the tops look dry. Cool on the baking sheet 1 minute before removing to a wire rack to cool completely.

For the icing, in a medium bowl beat the cream cheese, butter, orange peel, and orange juice until creamy. Beat in the confectioners' sugar until blended and smooth. Spread about 1$\frac{1}{2}$ teaspoons of the icing on each cookie. Sprinkle with the chopped walnuts. Let the icing set 1 to 2 hours.

Makes 4 dozen cookies

Mary Louise Moore, Queen Mama

Fayette-Greene Mama Mias,
Uniontown, Pennsylvania

Crispy Oatmeal Cookies

1$\frac{1}{2}$ cups quick-cooking oats	$\frac{1}{2}$ teaspoon baking soda
$\frac{1}{2}$ cup all-purpose flour	$\frac{1}{2}$ cup melted shortening
$\frac{1}{2}$ cup firmly packed light or dark brown sugar	2 tablespoons hot water

Preheat the oven to 350 degrees. Grease a baking sheet. Set aside.

In a large bowl combine the oats, flour, brown sugar, and baking soda, mixing well. Add the shortening and hot water. Mix well. Drop by $\frac{1}{2}$ teaspoons onto the prepared baking sheet. Bake 10 to 12 minutes, or until golden brown. Remove from baking sheet and cool on wire racks.

Makes 6 dozen small cookies

Marilyn Puett, Divine Miss M

Red Hat Rovers,
Huntsville, Alabama

Crispy Lemon Cookies

1 (18.25-ounce) package lemon cake mix	1/2 cup (1 stick) butter or margarine, melted
1 cup crisp rice cereal	1 large egg, lightly beaten

Preheat the oven to 350 degrees. In a large bowl combine the cake mix, cereal, butter, and egg, blending well. Form the dough into 1-inch balls. Place 2 inches apart on an ungreased cookie sheet. Flatten with a fork. Bake 9 to 12 minutes, or until very light golden brown around the edges. Cool 1 minute and remove to a cooling rack.

Makes 3 to 4 dozen cookies

Carlotta Wixon, Queen Mother

Sierra Sirens,
Grass Valley, California

Molasses Cookies

1 cup dark molasses	1/2 teaspoon cinnamon
1 cup firmly packed dark brown sugar	1/2 teaspoon nutmeg
1 cup vegetable shortening	5 cups all-purpose flour
1 teaspoon salt	1 cup water, divided
1 large egg	2 teaspoons baking soda
	Confectioner' sugar, for garnish

Preheat the oven to 350 degrees. Grease and flour 2 baking pans or line the pans with parchment paper. Set aside.

In a large bowl cream the molasses, brown sugar, and shortening. Add the salt, egg, cinnamon, and nutmeg. Add the flour alternately with 3/4 cup of the water. In a small bowl combine the baking soda and the remaining 1/4 cup water. Add to the batter.

Drop by tablespoonsful onto prepared pans and bake about 15 minutes. Dust with confectioners' sugar while still warm.

Makes 5 to 6 dozen cookies

Judy Sausto, Dame Judy
Dames with a Par-Tea Hat-titude,
Egg Harbor Township, New Jersey

Date Cookies

1 (8-ounce) package pitted dates, chopped	1 large egg, slightly beaten
1/2 cup flaked coconut	1 1/2 cups crisp rice cereal
1/2 cup sugar	1/2 cup chopped walnuts
1/4 cup (1/2 stick) butter	1 teaspoon vanilla
	Red and green sugars

In a large saucepan combine the dates, coconut, sugar, butter, and egg. Cook, stirring constantly, over medium-low heat 5 to 10 minutes, or until the mixture thickens and bubbles. Remove the saucepan from the heat and add the cereal, walnuts, and vanilla. Cool 10 minutes. Shape the cookies into balls. Keep fingers moist with butter. Roll in colored sugar and serve.

Makes 1 1/2 dozen cookies

Jean Davison, Red Hat Lady
Purple Passions,
Cincinnati, Ohio

Gayle's Famous Fruitcake Cookies

6 cups chopped pecans	1¼ cups chopped candied pineapple
2 cups graham cracker crumbs	¼ cup (½ stick) butter
1½ cups dark or golden raisins	½ cup canned evaporated milk
1¼ cups chopped red or green (or mixed) candied cherries	4½ cups mini-marshmallows
	1½ cups flaked coconut

In a large bowl combine the pecans, graham cracker crumbs, raisins, cherries, and pineapple, mixing well. In a large saucepan melt the butter. Add the evaporated milk and marshmallows. Cook over low heat, stirring constantly, until the marshmallows are melted. Pour over the mixture in the bowl and mix well.

Shape into 1-inch balls. Roll the balls in coconut and place on waxed paper until cool. Store in an airtight container.

Makes 7 to 8 dozen cookies

Gayle Whitehead Manning, Princess
Strawberry Red Hat Gals,
Lake Butler, Florida

Pistachio Thumbprint Cookies

COOKIE DOUGH:

- 1/3 cup confectioners' sugar
- 1 cup (2 sticks) butter or margarine, softened
- 1 teaspoon vanilla extract
- 3/4 teaspoon almond extract
- 1 (3.4-ounce) package instant pistachio pudding
- 1 large egg
- 2 cups all-purpose flour
- 11/4 cups finely chopped walnuts or pistachios

FILLING:

- 11/2 cups confectioners' sugar
- 1 teaspoon vanilla extract
- 2 tablespoons butter or margarine, softened
- 2 tablespoons milk

Preheat the oven to 350 degrees. Grease a cookie sheet. Set aside.

For the cookie dough, combine confectioners' sugar, butter, vanilla extract, almond extract, pudding mix, and egg; mix well. Stir in the flour. Shape into 1-inch balls. Roll balls in nuts and place 2 inches apart on cookie sheet. Make a thumbprint in each cookie. Bake 10 to 14 minutes, or until light golden brown. Cool 1 minute then transfer to a wire rack.

For the filling, combine the confectioners' sugar, vanilla extract, butter, and milk in a medium bowl. Fill the indentation of each cookie. Let the cookies stand on the wire rack until the filling is set. Store in an airtight container.

Makes 31/2 dozen cookies

Joann Mack, Goddess of Getaway
Dizzy Dames of Unknown Fame,
Clifton, New Jersey

Jubilee Jumbles

COOKIE DOUGH:

- 1/2 cup butter-flavored shortening
- 1 cup firmly packed light brown sugar
- 1/2 cup granulated sugar
- 2 large eggs
- 1 cup evaporated milk
- 1 teaspoon vanilla
- 2 1/4 cups all-purpose flour
- 1 teaspoon salt
- 1/2 teaspoon baking soda
- 1 cup chopped walnuts
- 1 cup chopped maraschino cherries

BURNT BUTTER GLAZE:

- 2 tablespoons butter
- 2 cups confectioners' sugar
- 1/4 cup evaporated milk

  Walnut and cherry halves, for garnish

For the cookie dough, in a large bowl cream the shortening, sugars, and eggs until creamy. Stir in the evaporated milk and vanilla.

In a medium bowl combine the flour, salt, and baking soda. Stir into the creamed mixture. Fold in the walnuts and cherries. Chill the dough for 1 hour.

Preheat the oven to 375 degrees. Grease 2 baking sheets. Drop the dough by teaspoonsful onto the prepared baking sheets. Bake 10 minutes.

For the glaze, heat the butter in a medium saucepan until golden brown. Add the confectioners' sugar and evaporated milk. Beat until smooth. Frost the warm cookies. Top with walnut and cherry halves.

Makes about 4 dozen cookies

Phyllis Jenkins, Queen Momma

Durham Dillies,
Durham, North Carolina

Maple Cream Delights

COOKIE DOUGH:
- 1 cup shortening or butter
- 1 teaspoon vanilla
- 1/2 teaspoon maple flavoring
- 2 cups firmly packed light brown sugar
- 2 large eggs
- 3¾ cups all-purpose flour

- 2 teaspoons baking soda
- 1 cup sour cream

FROSTING:
- 6 tablespoons butter
- 1 teaspoon maple flavoring
- 1/2 cup evaporated milk
- Confectioners' sugar

Preheat the oven to 350 degrees. Grease 2 cookie sheets. Set aside.

For the cookie dough, in a large bowl cream together the shortening, vanilla, maple flavoring, brown sugar, and eggs.

In a medium bowl combine the flour and baking soda. Add to the creamed mixture alternately with the sour cream, mixing well after each addition. Drop the dough by teaspoonsful onto the prepared cookie sheets. Bake 13 to 15 minutes, or until golden brown. Do not underbake.

For the frosting, in a medium saucepan melt the butter and cool to room temperature. Stir in the maple flavoring and evaporated milk. Stir in enough confectioners' sugar until the frosting is of a spreadable consistency. Cover the cooled cookies with a thick layer of frosting.

Makes about 3 dozen cookies

Dorothy M. Riley, Mistress of Fun and Adventure

Saguaro Sweethearts,
Green Valley, Arizona

Maurya's Lemon Chip Cookies

2/3 cup margarine, softened	1 1/4 cups all-purpose flour
3/4 cup sugar	1/2 teaspoon baking soda
1 large egg	1/2 teaspoon salt
1 teaspoon lemon extract	1 (6-ounce) package lemon chips

Preheat the oven to 225 degrees.

In a large bowl cream the margarine, sugar, egg, and lemon extract. Add the flour, baking soda, and salt, stirring until well mixed. Fold in the lemon chips. Drop by teaspoonsful onto an ungreased cookie sheet. Bake 10 minutes. Increase the oven temperature to 375 degrees and bake an additional 2 to 3 minutes. Cool the cookies on wire racks.

Makes 2 dozen cookies

Maurya Batten, Queen
Fantabulous Royal Rubies,
Charlottesville, Virginia

Southern Shortbread Cookies

1/2 cup (1 stick) butter, softened	1/8 teaspoon salt
5 tablespoons sugar	1/2 teaspoon vanilla
1 cup all-purpose flour	30 blanched whole almonds

Preheat the oven to 350 degrees. Lightly grease a cookie sheet.

In a large bowl cream the butter and sugar until fluffy. Add the flour and salt, mixing well. Stir in the vanilla.

Roll the dough into small balls and place on the prepared cookie sheet. Flatten each cookie and top with an almond. Bake 20 to 25 minutes, or until brown. Remove from the cookie sheet and cool on a wire rack.

Makes about 30 cookies

Marie Blitch, Queen

The Dixie Darlings,
Matthews, North Carolina

Mocha Latte Crinkles

1/3 cup butter, softened	1 teaspoon ground cinnamon
1 cup firmly packed brown sugar	2 large egg whites
2/3 cup unsweetened cocoa powder	1/3 cup low-fat vanilla yogurt
1 tablespoon instant coffee granules	1 1/2 cups all-purpose flour
1 teaspoon baking soda	1/4 cup granulated sugar

In a large mixing bowl cream the butter with an electric mixer on medium to high speed for 30 seconds. Add the brown sugar, cocoa powder, coffee granules, baking soda, and cinnamon. Beat until combined, scraping the sides of the bowl occasionally. Beat in the egg whites and yogurt until combined. Beat in as much of the flour as you can with the mixer. Stir in the remaining flour with a wooden spoon. Cover and chill the dough for 2 to 3 hours.

Preheat the oven to 350 degrees. Place the sugar in a small bowl. Drop the dough by teaspoonsful into the granulated sugar and roll into balls. Place the balls 2 inches apart on an ungreased cookie sheet. Bake 8 to 10 minutes, or until the edges are firm. Cool on wire racks.

Makes about 40 cookies

Deanna Farrell, Queen Mum
Pinehurst Rosebuds,
Honeyoye Falls, New York

Pineapple Vanilla Wafer Cookies

COOKIE DOUGH:

- 1/2 cup sugar
- 1/4 cup (1/2 stick) butter
- 1 large egg, well beaten
- 1/2 cup drained crushed pineapple, with 1/2 cup juice reserved
- 1/2 cup finely chopped walnuts
- 1 (12-ounce) box vanilla wafers

COATING:

- 1/2 cup sugar
- 1/4 cup (1/2 stick) butter
- 1 large egg, well beaten
- 1/2 cup reserved pineapple juice
  Flaked coconut

For the cookie dough, in a large saucepan combine the sugar, butter, egg, pineapple, and walnuts. Bring to a boil, and boil 5 minutes. Turn off the heat and let the mixture bubble a few minutes. Cool until thickened. Spread the mixture on the bottom of a vanilla wafer. Top with another wafer, making a sandwich. Repeat, using all of the cookies. Place on a cookie sheet and refrigerate overnight.

For the coating, in a medium saucepan combine the sugar, butter, egg, and the reserved pineapple juic. Bring the mixture to a boil, and boil 5 minutes. Turn off the heat and let the mixture bubble a few minutes. Refrigerate until completely cooled. Using your fingers, rub the coating all over the cookies. Roll the cookies in coconut. Place in the freezer to set.

Note: These cookies are better if you freeze them for a couple of days before you serve them.

Makes 12 servings

Niki Snedeger, HRH Princess Nic Dutchess of Ding-A-Ling

Red Hatted Madd Hatters,
West Valley City, Utah

Orange Almond Biscotti

¾ cup sugar
3 large eggs
¼ teaspoon salt
1 teaspoon vanilla extract
¼ teaspoon almond extract
2 cups all-purpose flour

1 teaspoon baking soda
2 tablespoons grated orange zest
1 cup sliced almonds
1 large egg white, beaten
Sugar for sprinkling

Preheat the oven 300 degrees. Line a baking sheet with parchment paper. Set aside.

In a large bowl cream the sugar, eggs, salt, and extracts on high speed with an electric mixer 6 minutes, or until thickened. In a small bowl combine the flour and baking soda. Add to the creamed mixture until all the ingredients are moistened.

Make a well in the center of the dough and add the orange zest and sliced almonds. Fold into the dough. Using a spatula, pour the dough onto the prepared baking sheet. Spread into a 16 x 4-inch flattened roll about ¾-inch thick. Brush the roll with the beaten egg white. Sprinkle with additional sugar.

Bake 1 hour, or until light brown. Remove from the oven and cool about 10 minutes. Reduce the oven temperature to 275 degrees. Using a bread knife, cut the biscotti crosswise into thin slices. Place the slices, cut side down, on the baking sheet. Bake for 10 minutes. Turn the biscotti over and bake an additional 10 minutes. Cool and store in an airtight container.

Makes 2 dozen biscotti

Sharon Simpson, Queen Mom
Ladies of the Lake,
Abbeville, Alabama

Chocolate Chip Orange Shortbread

1 cup confectioners' sugar	1/4 cup cornstarch
1 cup (2 sticks) butter, softened	1 1/2 cups miniature chocolate chips, divided
1 tablespoon grated orange peel	2 teaspoons shortening
1 3/4 cups all-purpose flour	

Preheat the oven to 325 degrees.

In a large bowl combine the confectioners' sugar and butter, beating until light and fluffy. Add the orange peel, blending well. Add the flour and cornstarch. Mix well. Stir in 3/4 cup of the chocolate chips.

Divide the dough into 4 equal portions. Shape each portion into a ball. On an ungreased cookie sheet, press or roll each ball into a 6-inch round, 1/4 inch thick. With a knife, score each round into 8 wedges. Prick each wedge three times with a fork. Bake 17 to 27 minutes, or until the edges are light golden brown. Cool 5 minutes. Prick again with a fork, and cut into the wedges. Remove the wedges from the cookie sheets and place on wire racks. Cool 15 minutes.

In a small saucepan over low heat, melt the remaining 3/4 cup chocolate chips and the shortening, stirring constantly. Dip the rounded end of the cooled shortbread wedges in the melted chocolate. Place on waxed paper or wire racks for the chocolate to set. Store in an airtight container.

Makes 2 1/2 dozen shortbread

Toni Whitehead, Queen
Crawford County Cuties,
Van Buren, Arkansas

Pumpkin Whoopie Pies

These make wonderful gifts.

COOKIE DOUGH:

- 2 cups firmly packed brown sugar
- 1 cup vegetable oil
- 1 1/2 cups canned pumpkin
- 1 teaspoon vanilla extract
- 2 large eggs, well beaten
- 3 1/2 cups all-purpose flour
- 1 1/2 teaspoons cinnamon
- 1 teaspoon baking soda
- 1 teaspoon baking powder
- 1 teaspoon salt
- 1/2 teaspoon ginger
- 1/2 teaspoon ground cloves
- 1/2 teaspoon nutmeg

FILLING:

- 1 large egg white
- 2 tablespoons milk
- 1 teaspoon vanilla extract
- 2 cups confectioners' sugar, divided
- 3/4 cup shortening

Preheat the oven to 350 degrees. Grease 2 cookie sheets.

For the cookie dough, in a large bowl cream the brown sugar and oil. Add the pumpkin, vanilla, and eggs.

In a medium bowl sift together the flour, cinnamon, baking soda, baking powder, salt, ginger, cloves, and nutmeg. Add to the pumpkin mixture and mix until well blended. Drop by tablespoonful onto the prepared cookie sheets, making sure you have an even number.

Bake 10 to 12 minutes. Cool completely.

For the filling, in a medium bowl mix the egg white, milk, vanilla, and 1 cup of the confectioners' sugar. Blend in the shortening and the remaining 1 cup of confectioners' sugar.

Place 1 heaping tablespoon of filling between two cookies. Wrap individually in plastic wrap, if desired.

Makes 3 dozen

Josephine Morrison, Queen Red Rover

Purple Playground Ladies,
Sand Springs, Oklahoma

As any woman can tell you—every fur has a story.

From L to R:
Jo Martyn, Dixie Johnson, Polly Anna Harris, Arlene Key, Dee Henning, Jane Garron, and Jan Michaelson.

Photo submitted by Jo Martyn, Nonpareils, Knoxville, Tennessee.

Raspberry Swirl Cookies

1 cup (2 sticks) butter, softened
2 cups sugar
2 large eggs, beaten
2 teaspoons pure vanilla extract
3¾ cups all-purpose flour
2 teaspoons baking powder

1/8 teaspoon kosher salt
1 (12-ounce) jar seedless raspberry jam
1 cup sweetened flaked coconut, finely chopped
1/2 cup pecans, finely chopped

In a large bowl cream the butter and sugar. Add the eggs and vanilla. Mix well.

In a small bowl combine the flour, baking powder, and salt. Add to the creamed mixture a little at a time. Mix well after each addition. Cover and chill for at least 2 hours.

Divide the dough in half. On a lightly floured surface, roll each half into a 13 x 9-inch rectangle. In a small bowl combine the jam, coconut, and pecans. Spread over the rectangles with a spatula. Carefully roll up into a jellyroll, starting with the long end. Wrap in plastic wrap. Refrigerate overnight.

Preheat the oven to 375 degrees. Line 2 cookie sheets with parchment paper.

Cut each roll into 1/3-inch slices. Place on the prepared cookie sheets and flatten slightly. Bake 10 to 12 minutes, or until lightly browned. Cool on wire racks.

Makes 6 dozen cookies

Carolyn Hardimon, The Recipe Lady
Elegant Swans,
Belleville, Illinois

Mouthwatering Bars and Luscious Brownies

Savored with fingers or forks

More dense than cake, more solid than pudding—brownies and bars are usually perfect for picking up with fingers. You can probably get away without a plate, but you are certain to need a napkin after you (discreetly) lick your fingers! No sense in wasting the tiniest delectable fraction of enjoyment, right?

Butterscotch Confetti Squares

Cooking spray
1/4 cup (1/2 stick) margarine
1/4 cup peanut butter

1 cup butterscotch chips
2 cups miniature colored marshmallows

Grease a 12 x 12-inch baking pan with cooking spray. Set aside.

In a large saucepan melt the margarine and peanut butter. Add the butterscotch chips and stir constantly until melted. Set the saucepan in cold water and stir quickly to cool slightly. Add the marshmallows, 1/2 cup at a time. Work quickly, as the mixture hardens fast. Spoon the mixture into the prepared pan and press into the pan evenly. Score the top of the mixture into 11/2-inch pieces and refrigerate.

Makes about 5 dozen

Gay Mentes, Growl Tigggerr X Pinky
Red Hot Jazzy Ladies,
Kelowna, British Columbia

Caramel Squares

2 cups baking mix
2 cups rolled oats
1½ cups packed dark brown sugar
½ cup (1 stick) butter, melted
1 (14-ounce) package caramels

1/3 cup milk
1 (12-ounce) bag semisweet chocolate chips
1 cup chopped walnuts

Preheat the oven to 350 degrees.

In a large bowl combine the baking mix, oats, and brown sugar. Stir in the butter until the mixture is crumbly. Press half the mixture into a 13 x 9-inch baking pan. Bake 10 minutes.

In a 2-quart saucepan heat the caramels and milk over low heat, stirring constantly until smooth. Sprinkle the chocolate chips and walnuts over the baked layer. Drizzle the caramel mixture over the nuts. Pour the remaining crumbly mixture over the caramel, and press lightly. Bake 15 to 20 minutes, or until golden brown. Cut into squares while warm. Cool completely before removing from the pan.

Makes 2 dozen

Joanne Thill, Queen Mum
London Bridge Red Hots,
Lake Havasu City, Arizona

Chewy Pecan Pie Squares

1 (18.25-ounce) package yellow cake mix

5 large eggs, divided

1/3 cup vegetable oil

1 cup dark corn syrup

1 cup sugar

1/4 cup (1/2 stick) butter, melted

2 cups pecans, chopped

Preheat the oven to 350 degrees. Grease a 13 x 9-inch pan. Set aside.

In a large bowl, combine the cake mix, 1 of the eggs, and the salad oil until crumbly. Press into the bottom of the prepared pan. Bake 20 minutes.

In a large bowl beat the remaining 4 eggs with the corn syrup, sugar, and butter on medium speed with an electric mixer until blended. Stir in the pecans. Pour over the crust in the pan. Bake 45 minutes. Cool completely. Cut into 2-inch squares to serve.

Makes 2 dozen

Joan Kania, Princess
Hat'Attudes of Safety Harbor,
Clearwater, Florida

Peanutty Chewy Bars

1 (18-ounce) roll refrigerated sugar cookie dough	2 teaspoons vanilla
3 cups miniature marshmallows	1 (10-ounce) package peanut butter chips
2/3 cup corn syrup	2 cups crisp rice cereal
1/4 cup (1/2 stick) butter or margarine	2 cups salted peanuts

Preheat the oven to 350 degrees.

Break the cookie dough into pieces on an ungreased 13 x 9-inch baking pan. With floured fingers, press the dough evenly into the bottom of the pan to form a crust. Bake 15 to 20 minutes, or until light golden brown.

Remove the partially baked crust from the oven. Sprinkle the marshmallows evenly over top. Bake until the marshmallows just begin to puff. Remove from the oven and cool.

In a large saucepan heat the corn syrup, butter, vanilla, and peanut butter chips over medium heat, stirring constantly, until the mixture is smooth. Remove from the heat. Stir in the cereal and peanuts. Spoon the warm topping over the marshmallows, spreading evenly. Refrigerate about 45 minutes or until firm. Cut into 36 squares.

Makes 36 bars

Kim Mears, Queen Clumsy Coral
R.E.D. Real Elegant Ladies and Ruby Rascals,
Amherst, Ohio

Walnut Tea Squares

CRUST:

3/4 cup butter, softened

1/3 cup sugar

2 large egg yolks, well beaten

11/2 cups all-purpose flour

1 teaspoon vanilla extract

TOPPING:

2 tablespoons all-purpose flour

1/2 teaspoon baking powder

11/2 cups sugar

1/4 teaspoon salt

2 large eggs, beaten

1/2 cup chopped walnuts

1 cup flaked coconut, moistened with a small amount of milk

1 teaspoon vanilla, lemon, or almond extract

Preheat the oven to 350 degrees.

For the crust, in a medium bowl beat the butter with an electric mixer. Blend in the sugar. Add the beaten egg yolks, flour, and vanilla, mixing well. Spoon the batter into a 9 x 9-inch pan. Bake 12 minutes, or until the crust is light brown.

Prepare the topping while the crust is baking. In a medium bowl combine the flour, baking powder, sugar, and salt. Stir in the eggs, walnuts, coconut, and extract, mixing well. Spread the mixture over the crust. Bake 20 minutes. Cool and cut into squares.

Makes 16 squares

Reyes Smith, Queen
Carefree Crimson Court of Coventry,
Royal Oak, Michigan

White Chocolate Cranberry Bars

PASTRY:

1 (7-ounce) block frozen puff pastry, thawed
1 tablespoon sugar
1 teaspoon cinnamon

FILLING:

10 (1-ounce) squares white chocolate
1 cup sour cream
1/2 cup (1 stick) butter or margarine
1 cup chopped cranberries, fresh or frozen

Preheat the oven to 375 degrees. Grease a 15 x 12-inch jelly-roll pan.

For the pastry, roll the puff pastry into a 15 x 10-inch rectangle. Place in the prepared pan. Sprinkle the pastry with the sugar and cinnamon. Bake for 30 minutes, or until golden brown.

For the filling, using an oven-safe bowl, combine the white chocolate, sour cream, butter, and cranberries. Place the bowl in the oven for 5 minutes, or until the chocolate is soft. Remove the bowl from the oven and stir the mixture until smooth. (Or if you prefer, you can melt the chocolate with the other ingredients in a double boiler over low heat on the stove for 5 minutes.)

When the pastry is removed from the oven, use a spoon to crack the puffed surface so it is level. Pour the filling over the hot pastry. Let cool and then refrigerate overnight. Cut into 12 pieces. Serve chilled.

Makes 12 bars

Joyce Wigle, Lady Joyce of Diamond
Scarlett Shady Ladies,
Wheatley, Ontario

Apple Nut Squares

3 large eggs	1/4 teaspoon salt
1¾ cups sugar	4 to 6 apples (McIntosh preferred), peeled and chopped
1 cup vegetable oil	1 cup chopped nuts
2 cups all-purpose flour	Confectioners' sugar (optional)
1 teaspoon baking soda	
1 teaspoon cinnamon	

Preheat the oven to 350 degrees. Lightly grease a 13 x 9-inch baking pan.

In a large bowl, blend the eggs, sugar, and oil. Set aside.

In a medium bowl, combine the flour, baking soda, cinnamon, and salt. Combine the flour mixture with the egg mixture and stir until thoroughly mixed. Fold in the apples and nuts and mix thoroughly. Spoon into the prepared pan. Bake 50 to 60 minutes, or until a wooden pick comes out clean. Cool and cut into squares. Sprinkle with confectioners' sugar, if desired.

Makes 2 dozen

Patt MacLellan, Princess Ladybug

Red Bonnet Sisters,
Lakeland, Florida

Lemon–Glazed Persimmon Bars

BARS:

1 1/2 teaspoons lemon juice
1 cup persimmon pulp
1 teaspoon baking soda
1 large egg
1 cup sugar
1/2 cup vegetable oil
3/4 cup chopped dates
1 3/4 cups all-purpose flour

1 teaspoon salt
1 teaspoon cinnamon
1 teaspoon nutmeg
1/3 teaspoon cloves
1 cup chopped walnuts and pecans

LEMON GLAZE:

1 cup confectioners' sugar
2 tablespoons lemon juice

Preheat the oven to 350 degrees. Grease and flour a 13 x 10-inch jelly-roll pan. Set aside.

For the bars, in a medium bowl combine the lemon juice and persimmon pulp. Stir in the baking soda and set aside.

In a large bowl, lightly beat the egg, and then stir in the sugar, oil, and dates.

In a small bowl combine the flour, salt, cinnamon, nutmeg, and cloves.

Stir the flour mixture into the egg mixture alternately with the persimmon mixture. Stir in the nuts until evenly mixed.

Pour the mixture into the prepared pan. Bake 25 minutes. Cool in the pan on a wire rack 5 minutes.

For the lemon glaze, in a small bowl combine the confectioners' sugar and lemon juice. Drizzle over the bars and cut into individual servings.

Makes 12 to 15 servings

Patricia Hauenstein, Queen Mum Chickadee
Red Feather Dusters of Amboy,
Amboy, Illinois

Cranberry Nut Bars

6 large eggs	1 (12-ounce) package fresh cranberries
3 cups sugar	
3 cups all-purpose flour	1/2 cup chopped walnuts
1 cup (2 sticks) butter or margarine, melted	

Preheat the oven to 350 degrees. Grease a 13 x 9-inch baking pan.

In a large bowl beat the eggs until thickened. Gradually add the sugar, beating until thoroughly blended. Stir in the flour and butter. Blend well. Stir in the cranberries and walnuts, mixing gently just until combined. Pour into the prepared pan. Bake 60 minutes or until golden brown. Cool and cut into squares.

Makes 18 squares

Diane Vallier, Member
Red Raspberry Tarts,
Peetz, Colorado

Diva Date Bars

1 cup chopped dates	1/2 teaspoon salt
1 cup chopped prunes	1 cup whole-wheat flour
1 cup raisins	1 cup chopped nuts
1/2 cup (1 stick) butter or margarine	1/2 teaspoon cinnamon
1 cup cold water	1/4 teaspoon nutmeg
2 large eggs	Confectioners' sugar (optional)
1 teaspoon baking soda	

Preheat the oven to 350 degrees.

In a saucepan combine the dates, prunes, raisins, butter, and water. Bring the mixture to a boil over medium heat. In a large bowl mix the eggs, baking soda, salt, flour, nuts, cinnamon, and nutmeg. Stir in the date mixture. Pour into an 11 x 7-inch pan, and bake 30 minutes. Cool and sprinkle with confectioners' sugar, if desired, before serving. The date bars can be frozen.

Makes 12 servings

Linda Lee Parker,
Royal Highness, Skye O'Malley
Roswell Red Hots,
Roswell, Georgia

Raspberry Squares

¾ cup (1½ sticks) butter or margarine, softened	½ teaspoon baking powder
1 cup sugar	¼ teaspoon salt
1 large egg	1 cup chopped flaked coconut
1 teaspoon vanilla	½ cup chopped nuts
2 cups plus 1 tablespoon all-purpose flour	1 (12-ounce) jar raspberry preserves

Preheat the oven to 350 degrees. Grease and flour a 9 x 9-inch pan.

In a large bowl cream the butter and sugar. Add the egg and vanilla.

In a medium bowl combine the flour, baking powder, and salt. Add to the liquid batter. Stir in the coconut and nuts. (The batter will be very thick.)

Spoon about two-thirds of the batter into the prepared pan. Spread the preserves over it. Spoon the remaining batter on top.

Bake for 35 to 45 minutes or until golden.

Makes 15 squares

Cheri Evans, Dowager Duchess of Parmesan

Belle City Bellas,
Racine, Wisconsin

Simple Pearlicious Custard Bars

CRUST:

1/2 cup (1 stick) butter

1/3 cup sugar

3/4 cup all-purpose flour

1/4 teaspoon vanilla extract

TOPPING:

1 (8-ounce) package cream cheese, softened

1/2 cup plus 1/2 teaspoon sugar

1 large egg

1/2 teaspoon vanilla extract

1 (15 1/4-ounce) can pear halves, drained and sliced

1/2 teaspoon ground cinnamon

Preheat the oven to 350 degrees. Grease a 9 x 9-inch baking pan. Set aside.

For the crust, cream the butter and sugar. Mix in the flour and vanilla until well combined. Press the dough into the prepared pan. Bake 20 minutes or until lightly browned. Cool on a wire rack. Increase the oven temperature to 375 degrees.

For the topping, in a medium bowl beat the cream cheese until smooth. Add 1 cup of the sugar, the egg, and vanilla, beating until well combined. Pour over the crust.

Arrange pears in a single layer over cream cheese mixture. Combine the cinnamon and remaining sugar and sprinkle over pears. Bake 30 minutes. Cool on wire rack 45 minutes. Refrigerate 2 hours before cutting.

Makes 16 to 20 bars

Lena Caswell, Madam Cracker
Traveling Cooks with Hattitude,
Greenfield, Indiana

Apricot Squares

1 cup (2 sticks) butter or margarine, softened	2 cups firmly packed light brown sugar
1/2 cup sugar	4 large eggs
2 2/3 cups all-purpose flour, divided	1 teaspoon vanilla extract
1 teaspoon baking powder	2 (16-ounce) packages dried apricots
1/2 teaspoon salt	Sifted confectioners' sugar

Preheat the oven to 350 degrees. Line a 15 x 12-inch baking pan with parchment paper or aluminum foil, with the ends hanging over for easy removal of bars. Set aside.

In a large bowl mix the butter, sugar, and 2 cups of the flour until smooth. Press into the pan. Bake 25 minutes, or until light brown. Remove from the oven and cool.

In a large bowl combine the remaining flour, baking powder, and salt. Set aside. In a medium bowl cream the brown sugar, eggs, and vanilla. Stir into the flour mixture.

In a medium saucepan combine the apricots and a small amount of water and cook until soft. Cool and then chop into small pieces. Stir the apricots into the batter and spread the mixture over the baked layer. Bake 30 to 40 minutes, or until a wooden pick inserted in the center comes out clean. Cool and then cut into small squares. Dust with confectioners' sugar.

Note: You may need to use a hot, wet knife blade to cut the squares cleanly.

Makes 2 dozen

Barbara Bellerdine, Queen
Sophisticated Red Hat Ladies,
Auburn, New York

Carrot Bars

BARS:

2 cups sugar

1½ cups vegetable oil

4 large eggs

3 (4-ounce) jars baby food carrots

2½ cups all-purpose flour

1 teaspoon salt

2 teaspoons baking soda

2 teaspoons cinnamon

½ cup chopped nuts (optional)

FROSTING:

1 (3-ounce) package cream cheese, softened

¼ cup (½ stick) butter or margarine, softened

1 teaspoon vanilla

2 cups confectioners' sugar, sifted

Preheat the oven to 350 degrees. Grease and flour a 13 x 9-inch pan.

For the bars, in a large bowl combine the sugar, oil, eggs, carrots, flour, salt, baking soda, cinnamon, and nuts, if desired. Mix well. Pour into the prepared pan. Bake 30 to 40 minutes, or until a wooden pick inserted in the center comes out clean. Cool completely before frosting.

For the frosting, in a medium bowl beat together the cream cheese, butter, and vanilla until fluffy. Gradually add the confectioners' sugar, beating until smooth. Frost the bars.

Makes 24 bars

Darlene Rugenstein, Leading Lady
Scarlet Ladies of Tri-Cities,
Saginaw, Michigan

Pumpkin Bars

2   cups all-purpose flour
2   teaspoons baking powder
2   teaspoons ground cinnamon
1   teaspoon baking soda
1/4 teaspoon salt
4   large eggs
1   (15-ounce) can pumpkin
1   cup sugar
1   cup vegetable oil
3/4 cup chopped pecans

FROSTING:

1   (3-ounce) package cream cheese, softened
1/4 cup (1/2 stick) butter or margarine, softened
1   teaspoon vanilla
2   cups confectioners' sugar, sifted
24 pecan halves (optional)

Preheat the oven to 350 degrees.

In a medium bowl stir together the flour, baking powder, cinnamon, baking soda, and salt. In a large mixing bowl, beat together the eggs, pumpkin, sugar, and oil. Add the flour mixture and beat well until combined. Stir in the chopped pecans.

Spread the batter in an ungreased 13 x 9-inch baking pan. Bake 25 to 30 minutes, or until a toothpick inserted in the center comes out clean. Cool on a wire rack.

For the frosting, in a medium bowl beat together the cream cheese, butter, and vanilla until fluffy. Gradually add the confectioners' sugar, beating until smooth. Frost the bars. Top with pecan halves, if desired. Cut into squares. Store in the refrigerator.

Makes 24 bars

Pat Utterback, Princess Patrice

Siena Ya Ya Girls,
Las Vegas, Nevada

Chocolate In-Betweens

1 cup firmly packed brown sugar

3/4 cup (1 1/2 sticks) butter or margarine, chilled and cut into 8 pieces

1/2 teaspoon salt

1 1/2 cups all-purpose flour

1 cup quick oats

1 (14-ounce) can sweetened condensed milk

1 (6-ounce) package semisweet chocolate chips

Preheat the oven to 350 degrees. Grease a 13 x 9-inch baking pan. Set aside.

Using the steel blade of a food processor, combine the brown sugar, butter, and salt. Process to mix for 15 seconds (the mixture will be lumpy). Add the flour and oats. Pulse 2 to 3 times. Scrape the side of the bowl with a spoon. Repeat pulsing until the mixture is crumbly.

Press 2 1/2 cups of the mixture into the bottom of the prepared baking pan.

In a 2-quart saucepan combine the condensed milk and chocolate chips. Cook over low heat, stirring constantly, just until the chips melt. Pour over the crust in the pan, spreading evenly. Cover with the remaining crumb mixture. Bake 25 to 30 minutes, or until lightly browned. When cool, cut into bars.

Makes 24 to 30 bars

Pat Wick, Queen Mum

Wecandogals,
Gowanda, New York

Chocolate Chip Cheese Squares

1 (18-ounce) roll refrigerated chocolate chip cookie dough	1 1/2 cups sugar
2 (8-ounce) packages cream cheese, softened	2 large eggs
	1/2 teaspoon vanilla

Preheat the oven to 350 degrees.

Slice the cookie dough in half. Slice one of the halves into 1/4-inch pieces and arrange in a 13 x 9-inch baking pan. Press together to cover the bottom of the pan.

In a large bowl combine the cream cheese, sugar, eggs, and vanilla with an electric mixer. Pour over the cookie dough in the pan.

Slice the remaining half of the cookie dough roll into pieces, and place as close together as possible on top of the cream cheese mixture. (If needed, break some pieces of the dough to fill in large spaces.) Bake 30 to 35 minutes or until browned. Cool and then cut into squares.

Makes 12 to 15 squares

Judi Wilcox, May Flower
Jamaice Bay YaYa's,
Fort Myers, Florida

Texas Yum-Yums

1 cup all-purpose flour	1 cup confectioners' sugar
1/2 cup (1 stick) margarine, softened	1 (5.1-ounce) box instant chocolate pudding
1 cup finely chopped pecans	1 (3.9-ounce) box instant vanilla pudding
1 (12-ounce) container dessert whipped topping, divided	2 1/2 cups milk
1 (8-ounce) package cream cheese, softened	1 (1.55-ounce) chocolate bar, grated

Preheat the oven to 350 degrees.

In a medium bowl combine the flour, margarine, and pecans. Press into bottom of 13 x 9-inch glass baking dish. Bake 15 to 20 minutes, or until a wooden pick inserted in the middle comes out clean. Let cool.

In a medium bowl combine 1 cup of the whipped topping, the cream cheese, and confectioners' sugar. Spoon the mixture over the baked pecan crust.

In a large bowl beat the pudding mixes with the milk until firm consistency, and spoon over the cream cheese layer. Top with the remaining whipped topping and the grated chocolate. Cut into squares to serve.

Makes 24 servings

Myrna Devore, Vice Queen Lady of the Cats
Fluffy Not Stuffy Red Hatters,
San Antonio, Texas

Buttercream Brownies

BROWNIE:

1/2 cup (1 stick) butter

2 (1-ounce) squares unsweetened baking chocolate

1 cup sugar

2 large eggs

3/4 cup all-purpose flour

FILLING:

4 cups confectioners' sugar

2 (3-ounce) packages cream cheese, softened

6 tablespoons butter, softened

2 teaspoons vanilla extract

TOPPING:

1 (1-ounce) square unsweetened baking chocolate, melted

Preheat the oven to 350 degrees. Grease an 8 x 8-inch baking pan.

For the brownie, in a 2-quart saucepan melt the butter and chocolate over medium heat, stirring constantly, 4 to 6 minutes, or until smooth. Stir in the sugar, eggs, and flour until well blended. Spread into the prepared pan. Bake 25 to 30 minutes, or until the brownie begins to pull away from the sides of the pan. Cool on a wire rack.

For the filling, in a small bowl combine the confectioners' sugar, cream cheese, butter, and vanilla extract. Beat at medium speed, scraping the bowl often, until creamy. Spread over the cooled bars. Drizzle with the melted chocolate.

Makes 25 brownies

Donna Britton, Queen CoCo

Red Hot Glitz,
Frankfort, Kentucky

Tailgate Margarita Bars

2 cups plus 4 tablespoons all-purpose flour, divided	1 (10-ounce) can frozen margarita mix, thawed
1/2 cup confectioners' sugar	1/2 cup water
1 cup (2 sticks) butter, softened and cut into chunks	Zest of 1 lemon
	Zest of 1 lime
4 large eggs	Sweetened flaked coconut, toasted
	Lime peel, for garnish (optional)

Preheat the oven to 350 degrees. Line the bottom and sides of a 13 x 9-inch pan with aluminum foil.

In large bowl combine 2 cups of the flour and the confectioners' sugar. Add the butter, stirring just until the mixture is crumbly. Press the mixture into the bottom of the prepared pan. Bake 20 to 25 minutes, or until the crust starts to turn golden brown. Place the pan on a wire rack and cool completely.

In large bowl combine the remaining 4 tablespoons of flour, the eggs, margarita mix, water, and lemon and lime zests. Whisk the mixture together to combine completely. Pour the mixture over the cooled crust. Bake 15 to 20 minutes, or until the top is set. Cool completely on a wire rack. Sprinkle with coconut. Cut into bars. Garnish with strips of lime peel before serving, if desired

Makes 24 bars

Carolyn Rogers, Queen Mum
Royal Reds,
Knoxville, Tennessee

Marvelous Marbled Brownies

2   (4-ounce) packages dark chocolate

10 tablespoons butter, divided, softened

2   (3-ounce) packages cream cheese, softened

2   cups sugar, divided

6   large eggs, divided

1   cup plus 2 tablespoons flour

3   teaspoons vanilla, divided

1   teaspoon baking powder

1/2 teaspoon salt

1   cup coarsely chopped walnuts or pecans

1/2 teaspoon almond extract

In a microwave-safe dish, melt the chocolate and 6 tablespoons of the butter in the microwave, stirring to mix. Set aside to cool.

Preheat the oven to 350 degrees. Grease a 13 x 9-inch baking pan.

In a medium bowl cream the remaining butter and the cream cheese. Gradually add 1/2 cup of the sugar, creaming until light and fluffy. Blend in 2 of the eggs, 2 tablespoons of the flour, and 1 teaspoon of the vanilla. Set aside.

In a large bowl beat remaining eggs until thick and light in color. Gradually add remaining sugar, beating until thickened. Add baking powder, salt, and remaining flour. Blend in the chocolate mixture, nuts, almond extract, and remaining vanilla. Set 2 cups of chocolate batter aside. Spread remaining chocolate batter into pan. Top with the cream cheese mixture. Drop reserved chocolate batter by tablespoonsful onto cream cheese mixture and swirl with a spatula to marble. Bake 35 to 40 minutes. Cool and cut into squares.

Makes 24 brownies

Judy Sheppard, Loquacious Quipster
Honeys with Hattitude,
Hornell, New York

Ginny Hanley's Triple Chocolate Brownies

1   (4-ounce) package chocolate pudding (not instant)

1   (18.25-ounce) package dark chocolate cake mix

1   (6-ounce) package chocolate chips

1/2 cup chopped walnuts (optional)

Preheat the oven to 350 degrees. Grease and flour a 13 x 9-inch baking pan.

Prepare the pudding according to the package directions. In a medium bowl combine the prepared pudding with the cake mix. Beat about 2 minutes.

Pour the mixture into the prepared pan and spread evenly. Sprinkle the chocolate chips over the mixture, gently pressing the chips into the mixture. If desired, sprinkle the walnuts evenly, pressing in as well. Bake 30 minutes, or until a toothpick inserted in the center comes out clean. Refrigerate in the pan until chilled. Cut before serving.

Makes 24 brownies

Judith A. Yanarelli, Filly of Finance

Dizzy Dames of Unknown Fame,
Clifton, New Jersey

Krispie Brownies

1 (21.2-ounce) box brownie mix	1 cup semisweet or milk chocolate chips
1 (7-ounce) jar marshmallow crème	1 cup butterscotch chips
1/4 cup shaved paraffin	3 cups crisp rice cereal
1 cup peanut butter chips	

Preheat the oven to 350 degrees.

Prepare the brownies according to the package directions. Bake in a 13 x 9-inch pan. Let cool.

Spread the marshmallow crème on top of the brownies. In a large saucepan over low heat, melt the paraffin. Add the peanut butter, chocolate, and butterscotch chips, stirring constantly until melted. Remove the saucepan from the heat and stir in the rice cereal. Spread the mixture on top of the marshmallow crème. Chill in refrigerator. Cut into squares to serve.

Makes 15 to 20 brownies

Linda Pennington, Queen Bunny

Sassy Hattitudes,
Loganville, Georgia

Chocolate Mint Brownies

BOTTOM LAYER:
- 1 cup sugar
- 1/2 cup (1 stick) butter, softened
- 4 large eggs, beaten
- 1 cup all-purpose flour
- 1/2 teaspoon salt
- 1 (16-ounce) can chocolate syrup
- 1 teaspoon vanilla extract
- 1/2 cup chopped nuts

MIDDLE LAYER:
- 2 cups confectioners' sugar
- 1/2 cup (1 stick) butter, softened
- 2 tablespoons crème de menthe

TOP LAYER:
- 1 cup semisweet chocolate chips
- 6 tablespoons butter

Preheat the oven to 350 degrees. Line a 13 x 9-inch baking pan with parchment paper.

For the bottom layer, in a large bowl combine sugar, butter, eggs, flour, salt, chocolate syrup, vanilla, and nuts. Press into pan. Bake 30 minutes.

For the middle layer, in a medium bowl mix the confectioners' sugar, butter, and crème de menthe. Spoon over the cooled brownies.

For the top layer, in a small saucepan mix the chocolate chips and butter over low heat, stirring constantly. Let cool slightly. Spread over the middle layer. Chill thoroughly. Use the edges of the parchment paper to remove the brownies from the pan for easier cutting. Keep in the refrigerator.

Makes 20 to 24 brownies

Mary Louise Moore, Queen Mama
Fayette-Greene Mama Mia's,
Uniontown, Pennsylvania

Buttermilk Brownies

BROWNIES:

1/2 cup (1 stick) butter

1/2 cup vegetable oil

1 cup water

2 cups sugar

2 cups all-purpose flour

1/4 cup unsweetened cocoa powder

1/2 teaspoon salt

11/2 teaspoons baking soda

1 cup buttermilk

2 large eggs

1 teaspoon vanilla extract

FROSTING:

1/2 cup (1 stick) butter

1/3 cup buttermilk

1 (1-pound) package confectioners' sugar

1/4 cup unsweetened cocoa powder

1 teaspoon vanilla extract

Preheat the oven to 350 degrees.

For the brownies, in a medium saucepan, combine the butter, oil, and water. Bring to a boil, stirring constantly. Let cool. Combine sugar, flour, cocoa powder, and salt. Add the cooled liquid mixture. In a small bowl mix baking soda and buttermilk. Add eggs and vanilla. Add to sugar mixture; mix well. Pour the batter into a 15 x 12-inch jelly-roll pan. Bake 20 to 25 minutes. Cool.

For the frosting combine butter, buttermilk, confectioners' sugar, cocoa powder, and vanilla; mix well. Frost the brownies.

Makes 36 brownies

Marti Gilbert, Floundering Founder Queen Mother

Baxter Babes,
Mountain Home, Arkansas

Kahlúa Brownies

2/3 cup butter or margarine, softened	1/2 teaspoon salt
2 cups sugar	1/2 teaspoon baking powder
3 large eggs	11/2 cups all-purpose flour
3 (1-ounce) squares unsweetened chocolate	1/2 to 3/4 cup Kahlúa Kahlúa (optional)

Preheat the oven to 350 degrees.

In a large bowl cream the butter and sugar. Add the eggs, one at a time, mixing thoroughly after each addition.

In a microwave-safe dish, heat the chocolate for 30 seconds, or until melted. Drizzle the melted chocolate into the butter mixture. Add the salt, baking powder, and flour. Drizzle the Kahlúa into the batter. Spoon the batter into a 9 x 9-inch baking pan and bake 30 minutes.

Remove the brownies from the oven and, if desired, immediately coat the top with extra Kahlúa using a new small paintbrush.

Makes 25 brownies

Nancy Clemons, Queen Mother Nancy
Luscious Ladies of League City,
League City, Texas

Red Hat Bourbon Brownies

BROWNIES:

1/3 cup butter
1/2 cup sugar
2 tablespoons water
1 cup semisweet chocolate chips
2 large eggs
1 teaspoon vanilla
1/4 cup all-purpose flour
1/4 teaspoon baking soda
1/4 teaspoon salt

1/2 cup chopped pecans
2 to 3 tablespoons bourbon

FROSTING:

3 tablespoons butter, softened
1 1/2 cups sifted confectioners' sugar
2 to 3 teaspoons milk
1/4 teaspoon vanilla
1 or 2 drops red food coloring
1 ounce semisweet chocolate, melted

Preheat the oven to 350 degrees. Grease an 8 x 8-inch baking pan.

For the brownies, in a large saucepan combine the butter, sugar, and water. Cook, stirring over medium heat, until just boiling. Add the chocolate chips and stir until melted. Remove from the heat and cool slightly. Stir in the eggs and vanilla, beating lightly. Stir in the flour, baking soda, salt, and pecans. Spread the batter into the prepared pan. Bake 20 minutes, or until the edges are set and begin to pull away from the side of pan. Using a fork, prick the warm brownies several times. Drizzle the bourbon evenly over the brownies. Cool in the pan.

For the frosting, beat the butter in a medium bowl with an electric mixer for 30 seconds. Gradually add the confectioners' sugar, beating well. Slowly beat in 2 teaspoons of the milk and the vanilla. If necessary, beat in the remaining milk to reach spreading consistency. Add the food coloring and spread over the brownies. Drizzle the melted chocolate over the frosting. Cut into squares.

Makes 16 to 20 brownies

Brenda Huff, Queen Runamuke

Sweet Magnolias,
Fredericksburg, Virginia

Blonde Brownies

1 cup all-purpose flour

1/2 teaspoon baking powder

1/2 teaspoon baking soda

1/2 teaspoon salt

1/2 cup chopped walnuts

1/2 cup unsweetened flaked coconut

1/3 cup butter

1 cup firmly packed light brown sugar

1 tablespoon water

1 large egg, lightly beaten

1 teaspoon vanilla extract

1 (6-ounce) package semisweet chocolate chips

Preheat the oven to 350 degrees. Grease a 9 x 9-inch baking pan.

In a large bowl mix the flour, baking powder, baking soda, salt, walnuts, and coconut.

In a medium saucepan melt the butter. Remove the pan from the heat and add the sugar and water. Cool the mixture, and then stir in the egg and vanilla. Gradually add to the flour mixture, stirring well. Spread into the prepared pan. Sprinkle the chocolate chips on top. Bake 20 to 25 minutes, or until a wooden pick inserted in the center comes out clean.

Makes 25 brownies

Vivian Wainwright, Royal Member
The Belles of Bridgewater,
Bridgewater, Connecticut

Orange Brownies

BROWNIES:

1 1/2 cups all-purpose flour
2 cups sugar
1 cup (2 sticks) butter, softened
4 large eggs
2 teaspoons pure orange extract
1 teaspoon grated orange zest

GLAZE:

1 cup confectioners' sugar
2 tablespoons orange juice
1 teaspoon grated orange zest

Preheat the oven to 350 degrees. Grease a 13 x 9-inch pan. Set aside.

For the brownies, in a large bowl stir together the flour and sugar. Add the butter, eggs, orange extract, and orange zest. Beat with an electric mixer until well blended. Pour the batter into the prepared pan and bake 30 minutes, or until light golden brown. Remove from the oven and pierce the brownies with a fork.

For the glaze, in a small bowl combine the confectioners' sugar, orange juice, and orange zest, stirring until smooth. Pour the glaze over the warm brownies. Cool and cut into squares.

Makes 24 brownies

Ann Schwenker, Lady Laughs a Lot
Blossom Street Belles,
Lexington, South Carolina

Old-Fashioned Favorites

Childhood memories from Grandma's kitchen

My husband's Grandma Florence was rarely seen without her apron. She really knew how to spread a table, and her house was always *the* place to be for Sunday dinner.

Her cooking may not have been fancy, by today's standards, but everything that came out of her kitchen rated a "10" in the taste test. Her desserts were always her pièce de résistance. And the very best of them were the old favorites—thanks to her special secret ingredient: love!

Mom's Brown Betty

BATTER:

1¼ cups all-purpose flour

2 teaspoons baking powder

1 teaspoon salt

¾ cup sugar

1 large egg

½ cup milk

1 teaspoon vanilla extract

¼ cup raisins (optional)

2 apples, peeled and cut in eighths

SAUCE:

¼ cup margarine

¼ cup firmly packed light brown sugar

½ teaspoon cinnamon

1 tablespoon margarine

Preheat the oven to 350 degrees. Coat a 9 x 9-inch baking dish with cooking spray.

In a large bowl mix the flour, baking powder, salt, sugar, egg, milk, vanilla, and raisins, if desired. Pour into the prepared baking dish. Lay the apples evenly on top of the batter.

In a medium saucepan melt the margarine. Add the brown sugar and cinnamon. Pour over the apples. Dot the top with the margarine. Bake 25 to 35 minutes. Serve warm or cool.

Makes 6 servings

Gay Mentes, Growl Tigggerr X Pinky
Red Hot Jazzy Ladies,
Kelowna, British Columbia

Bread Pudding with Whiskey Sauce

8 to 10 dried bread slices	**WHISKEY SAUCE:**
1/2 cup raisins (optional)	1/4 cup (1/2 stick) butter
4 large eggs, beaten	1/2 cup sugar
2 1/4 cups whole milk	1 large egg yolk, beaten
1/2 cup sugar	2 tablespoons water
1 tablespoon vanilla	2 tablespoon whiskey
1/2 teaspoon cinnamon	

Preheat the oven to 350 degrees.

Cut the bread into small cubes. Place on baking sheets and bake 10 minutes, or until lightly toasted. Toss the bread cubes and the raisins, if desired, in a greased 2-quart baking dish.

In a large bowl combine the eggs, milk, sugar, vanilla, and cinnamon, mixing well. Pour over the bread, making sure all of the bread is covered. Soak for 2 to 3 minutes. Bake, uncovered, 40 to 45 minutes, or until a knife comes out clean.

To make the sauce, melt the butter in a small saucepan. Add the sugar, egg yolk, and water. Cook at a full boil, stirring constantly, 3 to 4 minutes, or until the sugar dissolves. Remove the pan from the heat and stir in the whiskey. Strain the sauce. Serve with the bread pudding.

Makes 9 servings

Marge Wicks, Lady Chit Chat
Q-Tea's,
Scottsdale, Arizona

Classic Tiramisu

6 large egg yolks
1 1/4 cups sugar
1 1/4 cups mascarpone cheese
1 3/4 cups heavy cream
2 (3-ounce) packages ladyfingers
1/3 cup coffee liqueur

SWEETENED WHIPPED CREAM:

1/2 cup heavy cream
1 tablespoon confectioners' sugar
1/4 teaspoon vanilla extract
Unsweetened cocoa powder, for garnish
Chocolate curls, for garnish

In a medium bowl combine the egg yolks and sugar. Whip until thick and lemon colored, about 1 minute. Place in the top of a double boiler over boiling water. Reduce the heat to low and cook 8 to 10 minutes, stirring constantly. Remove from the heat. Add the mascarpone cheese, beating well.

In a medium bowl whip the heavy cream until stiff peaks form. Fold into the egg yolk mixture. Set aside. Line the bottom and side of a 3-quart bowl with the ladyfinger halves. Brush with the coffee liqueur. Spoon half of the egg yolk-cream mixture into the ladyfinger-lined bowl. Repeat the ladyfingers, coffee liqueur, and cream layers.

For the whipped cream, in a small bowl combine the heavy cream, confectioners' sugar, and vanilla. Whip until stiff peaks form. Garnish the tiramisu with the whipped cream, cocoa powder, and chocolate curls. Cover and refrigerate several hours or overnight.

Makes 10 to 12 servings

Sharon Moreland, Red Hat Stepchild
Red Hat Stepchild, Saucier, Mississippi

Red Hatters Crockpot Delight

1 (21-ounce) can cherry or apple pie filling

1 (18.25-ounce) package yellow cake mix

1/2 cup (1 stick) butter, melted

1/3 cup chopped walnuts (optional)

Frozen whipped topping, thawed, or ice cream (optional)

Place the pie filling in a 1 1/2-quart slow cooker. In a medium bowl combine the cake mix and butter (the mixture will be crumbly). Pour over the pie filling. Sprinkle with walnuts, if desired. Cook, covered, on low 2 to 3 hours. Serve in bowls with whipped topping or ice cream, if desired.

Makes 10 to 12 servings

Joanne Augenstein, Queen of Mirth and Merriment

Red Birds of a Feather,
Yellow Springs, Ohio

Ambrosia

1 (3.4-ounce) package strawberry gelatin

1 (3.4-ounce) package orange gelatin

1 (16-ounce) can fruit cocktail, drained

2 to 3 bananas, sliced

1 1/2 cups flaked coconut

Frozen whipped topping, thawed

2/3 cup chopped nuts

Prepare the gelatins according to the package directions. Pour each into a 9 x 9-inch pan. Chill until firm. Cut the gelatin into small cubes. In a large bowl combine the gelatins, fruit cocktail, bananas, and coconut. Fold in enough whipped topping to coat the ingredients. Sprinkle with the nuts.

Makes 25 servings

Beverly Collick, Vice Queen of Crafts

The Crafty Crimson Chapeaus,
Wolverine Lake, Michigan

Bananas Foster

1/2 cup (1 stick) butter	1/8 teaspoon salt
4 tablespoons dark brown sugar	2 ripe bananas
1 cup dark rum	1/4 cup cognac, warmed
1/2 cup curaçao	1 quart vanilla ice cream

In a large skillet melt the butter. Add the brown sugar and stir until dissolved. Add the rum, curaçao, and salt. Bring to a boil. Thinly slice the bananas and stir into the syrup. Cook until the mixture begins to boil and the bananas are just tender. Pour the warmed cognac over the mixture and carefully ignite. Stir until the flame is almost extinguished. Serve the warm sauce over the ice cream.

Makes 4 servings

Mary Morris, Vice Queen Mary

Herzog's Hellacious Heifers of Haughton,
Shreveport, Louisiana

Crockpot Fruit Crisp

6 cups peeled and sliced Gala apples	1 cup all-purpose flour
6 cups peeled and sliced pears	1 cup rolled oats (not instant)
1 cup dried cherries	3/4 cup firmly packed dark brown sugar
1/2 cup sugar	
1 tablespoon grated orange peel	1 teaspoon ground ginger
2 teapoons cinnamon, divided	1/4 teaspoon allspice
Dash of nutmeg	3/4 cup butter, softened

Coat the inside of a slow cooker with cooking spray.

In a large bowl mix the apples, pears, dried cherries, sugar, orange peel, 1 teaspoon of the cinnamon, and the nutmeg. Toss well. Pour into the slow cooker. In a medium bowl combine the flour, oats, brown sugar, the remaining 1 teaspoon cinnamon, the ginger, and allspice. Crumble the butter into the flour mixture. Mix with your hands until the mixture is crumbly. Sprinkle over the fruit and pat down. Cook, covered, on high 2 to 3 hours, checking for softness every 30 minutes after 2 hours. Serve warm with cream, whipped cream, or ice cream.

Makes 6 to 8 servings

Judy Roth, Queen Mum
Rockin Red Hatters,
Warner, South Dakota

Granny's Rice Pudding

10 cups whole milk	4 large egg yolks, beaten
2 cups rice	1 teaspoon vanilla
1 1/2 teaspoons salt	Cinnamon, for garnish
2 1/4 cups sugar	

In a large saucepan bring the milk to a boil. Add the rice and salt. Return to a boil and then lower the temperature. Simmer 35 minutes, stirring occasionally. Add the sugar and cook 2 minutes. Gradually add the egg yolks and simmer 3 minutes longer. Remove from the heat and add the vanilla. Pour into a large bowl or into individual serving bowls and sprinkle with cinnamon.

Makes 10 servings

Glennis Kidder, Queen Mother .
Dazzling Divas Red Hatters of the Orestimba,
Newman, California

Peach Crisp

1 (29-ounce) can sliced peaches, drained	¾ cup firmly packed dark brown sugar
1 cup baking mix	½ teaspoon cinnamon
	¼ cup (½ stick) butter, softened

Preheat the oven to 400 degrees. Arrange the peach slices in an ungreased 8 x 8-inch baking dish. Set aside. In a large bowl combine baking mix, brown sugar, and cinnamon, mixing well. Cut butter into the mixture with a pastry blender. Spoon batter over the peaches. Bake, uncovered, 18 to 20 minutes.

Makes 6 to 8 servings

Bernice Cornmesser, Clever Princess of Keystrokes
Dixie Delight,
Bartlett, Tennessee

Flaming Cherries Jubilee

1 (16-ounce) can pitted dark sweet cherries	½ teaspoon grated orange peel
¼ cup rum	½ teaspoon almond extract
¼ cup currant jelly	¼ cup brandy
	½ gallon vanilla ice cream

Drain the cherries, reserving ¼ cup of the juice. In a 1½-quart microwave-safe dish with lid, combine the cherries, the reserved juice, the rum, jelly, orange peel, and almond extract, mixing well. Microwave, covered, on high 5 to 6 minutes. Heat the brandy in the microwave 15 to 20 seconds.

Pour over the cherry mixture and ignite. Serve over the vanilla ice cream.

Makes 8 servings

Margaret Metz, Countess of Barter and Brides
The Hottie Red Hatters of Coralville,
Coralville, Iowa

Rhubarb Crunch

1	cup all-purpose flour	1	cup granulated sugar
1	cup firmly packed light brown sugar	1	cup water
3/4	cup oats	1	teaspoon vanilla
1	cup (1/2 stick) butter, melted	1	tablespoon cornstarch
4	cups diced rhubarb		

Preheat the oven to 350 degrees. Grease a 12 x 8-inch glass baking dish.

In a large bowl combine the flour, brown sugar, oats, and butter. Press three-fourths of the mixture into the bottom of the prepared dish. Spoon the rhubarb over the crust.

In a medium saucepan cook the granulated sugar, water, vanilla, and cornstarch, stirring until the mixture is clear. Pour over the rhubarb. Crumble the remaining flour mixture on top. Bake 1 hour. Serve with ice cream or whipped cream.

Makes 10 servings

Paula Rae Espy, Red Hat Accountess
Red Hot River Babes,
Burlington, Iowa

Old Southern Grated Sweet Potato Pudding

1/2 cup (1 stick) butter, softened	1 tablespoon ground allspice
1 cup cane syrup	1 tablespoon ground cinnamon
1 cup whole milk	1 cup heavy cream, whipped
4 cups grated sweet potatoes	1 cup raisins (optional)
1 teaspoon salt	3 large eggs, beaten
1/2 teaspoon ground cloves	

Preheat the oven to 375 degrees. Grease a 2-quart baking dish.

In a large bowl mix the butter, cane syrup, milk, sweet potatoes, salt, cloves, allspice, cinnamon, whipped cream, and raisins, if desired. Stir in the eggs. Pour the mixture into the prepared baking dish. Bake 40 minutes, stirring the crust to the middle as it forms on the edges. Do this several times during the baking process.

Note: This recipe can also be cooked all day on low heat in a slow cooker.

Serve warm.

Makes 4 to 6 servings

Lucinda Denton,
Founding Queen Mother
Nonpareils,
Knoxville, Tennessee

Cowboy Peach Cobbler

3 cups sliced peaches	1/2 teaspoon salt
1/4 cup plus 3 tablespoons sugar, divided	1 tablespoon baking powder
1 tablespoon lemon juice	1/3 cup shortening or soft margarine
1 teaspoon almond extract	1/2 cup milk
1 1/2 cups all-purpose flour	1 large egg

Preheat the oven to 350 degrees. Grease an 8 x 8-inch pan.

Arrange the peaches in the prepared pan. In a small bowl combine 1/4 cup of the sugar, the lemon juice, and almond extract. Sprinkle over the peaches. Bake 10 minutes.

In a medium bowl combine the flour, salt, baking powder, and 1 tablespoon of the sugar. Cut in the shortening until crumbly. Add the milk and egg. Stir just until moistened. Spread the batter over the hot peaches and sprinkle with the remaining 2 tablespoons sugar. Increase the oven temperature to 375 degrees. Bake the cobbler 40 minutes.

Makes 8 servings

Joyce Lauer, Princess Laffing Hatter
Ms. Astors Disasters,
Corpus Christi, Texas

Sticky Toffee Pudding

3 large egg whites
1/2 cup (1 stick) butter, softened
1/2 cup firmly packed dark brown sugar
1 teaspoon vanilla
11/4 cups all-purpose flour
11/2 teaspoons baking powder
1/2 teaspoon baking soda
1/2 teaspoon nutmeg
Pinch of salt

3/4 cup chopped dates
1/2 cup milk

CARAMEL SAUCE:

3/4 cup (11/2 sticks) butter
1 cup firmly packed dark brown sugar
1/2 cup whipping cream
2 tablespoons corn syrup

Preheat the oven to 350 degrees. Grease a 6-cup baking dish.

In a medium bowl beat the egg whites until stiff peaks form. Set aside.

In a large bowl cream the butter and brown sugar until fluffy. Stir in the vanilla. In a medium bowl mix the flour, baking powder, baking soda, nutmeg, salt, and dates. Add the dry ingredients alternately with the milk to the butter mixture.

Stir a dollop of the egg whites into the butter mixture, and then fold in the rest until slightly streaky. Pour the mixture into the prepared baking dish and cover with a buttered piece of foil. Place the baking dish in a Dutch oven and add water halfway up the bowl. Bake 55 minutes. If the center of the pudding is runny, bake 20 minutes longer and check again. Remove from the oven when the center is set.

While the pudding is baking, prepare the caramel sauce. In a medium saucepan melt the butter. Add the brown sugar, cream, and corn syrup. Stir over low heat until the mixture comes to a boil. Cool slightly.

Turn the pudding out onto a large platter, and poke holes in it with a chopstick. Top with enough caramel sauce to fill the holes. Serve warm with additional sauce.

Makes 6 servings

Shirley Murphy, Lady Smurf
Red Hat Divas,
Toronto, Ontario

Cherry Trifle Red Hat Dessert

1 (6-ounce) package cherry gelatin

2 cups boiling water

1 (21-ounce) can cherry pie filling.

1 (8-ounce) package cream cheese, softened

3 cups milk, divided

2 (3.4-ounce) packages instant vanilla pudding

1 (16-ounce) frozen pound cake, thawed and sliced

1 (8-ounce) container frozen whipped topping, thawed

Red sugar (optional)

Maraschino cherries (optional)

In a medium bowl mix the cherry gelatin with the boiling water, stirring until dissolved. Allow the gelatin to cool to room temperature, and then stir in the cherry pie filling. Chill in the refrigerator until almost set.

In a medium bowl mix the cream cheese with a few tablespoons of the milk and beat until smooth. Add the remaining milk and pudding mix. Beat on low speed with an electric mixer about 2 minutes.

In a glass compote dish, trifle dish, or glass bowl, layer the sliced pound cake, cherry gelatin mixture, and vanilla pudding mixture. Repeat the layers. Top with the whipped topping. Add red sugar and maraschino cherries, if desired. Refrigerate.

Makes 20 servings

Dorothy M. Riley, Mistress of Fun and Adventure

Saguaro Sweethearts,
Green Valley, Arizona

Chocolate Mousse

1 (1-ounce) envelope unflavored gelatin	1/2 cup confectioners' sugar
3 tablespoons cold water	3/4 cup granulated sugar
2 (1-ounce) squares unsweetened chocolate	1 teaspoon vanilla extract
	1/4 teaspoon salt
1 cup milk	2 cups heavy cream
	Chocolate shavings (optional)

In a large bowl soften the gelatin in the cold water and set aside.

In a double boiler melt the chocolate over hot water. Heat the milk just enough so that a film shows on the surface, and then slowly stir into the melted chocolate. Add the confectioner's sugar. Whisk until smooth. Cook, stirring constantly over low heat, until the mixture simmers. Remove from the heat and pour the chocolate mixture into the softened gelatin. Add the granulated sugar, vanilla, and salt, stirring well. Chill until slightly thickened, and then beat the mixture until light and airy. In a separate bowl, beat the heavy cream until it holds its shape. Fold into the chocolate mixture. Refrigerate in a serving bowl. Top with the chocolate shavings before serving, if desired.

Makes 6 to 8 servings

Sybil Longinotti
Red Hat Rogue Runners,
Grants Pass, Oregon

Chocolate Fondue with Brandy

1½ teaspoons cornstarch
1 tablespoon half-and-half
1½ teaspoons vegetable oil
½ teaspoon instant coffee granules
Dash of ground cinnamon
½ cup milk
½ cup semisweet chocolate chips
1 tablespoon brandy

1 loaf pound cake, cut into 1-inch cubes
1 (10-ounce) package mini marshmallows
1 banana, chopped
6 strawberries, chopped
2 slices pineapple, chopped
Chopped walnuts (optional)
Caramel topping (optional)

In the top of a double boiler, combine the cornstarch, half-and-half, and oil. Blend in the coffee granules, cinnamon, and milk. Cook over medium heat, stirring constantly, until slightly thickened. Add the chocolate chips and brandy. Cook, stirring constantly, until smooth. Transfer the mixture to a fondue pot or a chocolate fountain.

Serve with the pound cake cubes, marshmallows, and fruit for dipping. Top with walnuts and caramel if desired.

Makes 4 to 6 servings

Charlotte Beasley, Queen Charlotte B.

So. Belles of Boca Raton,
Boca Raton, Florida

Frozen Delights

Frosty palate pleasers

Brrrrrr! There's no getting around the fact that these treats are most enjoyable in the hotter times of the year. What could provide a more refreshing finale (or appetizer) to a summertime meal than an ice-cold, gloriously sweet dish of ice cream or frozen fluff? You get to cool off while you treat your taste buds. But, the Red Hat Society has no rules, and we advise enjoying an icy treat absolutely anytime it suits you! But don't dawdle over these dessert too long—they might melt!

Strawberry Ice Cream

1   pint whipping cream
1   (16-ounce) package frozen
    strawberries, thawed until icy
1   (5-ounce) can evaporated milk
1   (15-ounce) can sweetened
    condensed milk

1/2 cup sugar
1   tablespoon vanilla
    Whole milk

In a medium bowl beat the whipping cream until stiff peaks form. In a large bowl combine the strawberries, evaporated milk, condensed milk, sugar, and vanilla. Fold the whipped cream into the strawberry mixture. Pour the mixture into an ice cream maker and fill to the line with whole milk. Freeze according to the ice cream freezer manufacturer's directions.

Makes 1 gallon

Ina Starnes, Member

*Rambling Roses,
Gatesville, Texas*

Best-Ever Homemade Vanilla Ice Cream

4	cups whole milk	2	tablespoons pure vanilla
3	cups sugar	1/4	teaspoon salt
12	extra-large eggs, slightly beaten		Whole milk
4	(12-ounce) cans evaporated milk		

Scald the whole milk in a large saucepan. Remove from the heat and slowly mix in the sugar, eggs, evaporated milk, vanilla, and salt, whisking while pouring. Pour the mixture into an ice cream freezer. Add additional whole milk to fill to the line, if necessary. Freeze according to the ice cream freezer manufacturer's directions.

Makes 1 gallon

Elva Richard, Poppy Pal
Fluttering Butterflies,
Westminster, Colorado

Frozen Pistachio Cream Dessert with Ruby Raspberry Sauce

1 cup (about 27) crushed vanilla wafers

1/2 cup plus 2 tablespoons finely chopped red pistachios, divided

1/4 cup (1/2 stick) butter, melted

1 (3-ounce) package cream cheese, softened

1 (3 1/4-ounce) package instant pistachio pudding

1 1/4 cups milk

1 (8-ounce) carton frozen whipped topping, thawed

1 (10-ounce) package frozen raspberries, partially thawed

2 tablespoons sugar

2 tablespoons orange-flavored liqueur

In a medium bowl combine the wafers, 1/2 cup pistacios, and butter, blending well. Press mixture firmly into an ungreased 8 x 8-inch pan. In a separate bowl, beat the cream cheese until fluffy. Add pudding mix and milk, beating until smooth. Cover and refrigerate for 1 hour. Reserve 3/4 cup of whipped topping. Fold remaining whipped topping into cream cheese mixture. Spoon mixture into crust. Freeze 5 hours.

Before serving, allow the dessert to thaw in the refrigerator about 1 hour. Meanwhile, in a blender or food processor bowl, combine the raspberries, sugar, and liqueur. Blend until smooth. Strain to remove the seeds. To serve, garnish with the reserved whipped topping, the remaining pistachios, and the raspberry sauce.

Makes 9 servings

Mary Androff, Lady of Desserts
Razzle Dazzle of Clinton Township,
Warren, Michigan

Charlotte's Red Hat Baked Alaska

5 large egg whites	Chopped pecans
2/3 cup sugar	1 (10-ounce) package frozen strawberries, thawed
1 large sponge cake or angel food cake	1/4 cup Grand Marnier (optional)
1 cup Rocky Road, Heavenly Hash, or chocolate ice cream	

Preheat the oven to 450 degrees.

In a large bowl beat the egg whites until stiff peaks form. Gradually add the sugar.

Cut the cake into 4 rectangle slices. Place the ice cream and chopped pecans on each slice. Spread the meringue mixture to completely cover the ice cream. Bake until the meringue is light brown.

Mix the strawberries and their juice with the Grand Marnier, if desired. Drizzle over the meringue and serve.

Makes 2 to 4 servings

Charlotte Beasley, Queen Charlotte B.

So. Belles of Boca Raton,
Boca Raton, Florida

Rainbow Delight

1	pint whipping cream	1	cup chopped walnuts
3	tablespoons sugar	1	pint orange sherbet
1	teaspoon vanilla extract	1	pint lime sherbet
18	coconut macaroons	1	pint raspberry or lemon sherbet

In a large bowl whip the cream until stiff peaks form. Add the sugar and vanilla. Crush or grind the macaroons and mix with the walnuts. Fold the macaroon and nut mixture into the whipped cream. Put half the mixture into a 13 x 9-inch pan, and spread evenly. Drop the sherbets alternately by small teaspoonsful over the whipped cream making sure each flavor will be in each serving. Top with the remaining whipped cream mixture. Cover and freeze.

Makes 10 to 12 servings

Donnette Dulas, Princess of the Pennies

Crimson Cruisers,
Wells, Minnesota

Raspberry Fluff

CRUST:

1¹/₂ cups graham cracker crumbs

¹/₂ cup sugar

¹/₂ teaspoon cinnamon

¹/₃ cup melted butter

FILLING:

1 (8-ounce) package cream cheese, softened

¹/₄ cup confectioners' sugar

Pinch of salt

1 teaspoon vanilla

TOPPING:

1 (3.4-ounce) package strawberry gelatin

1 cup boiling water

1 tablespoon lemon juice

1 (12-ounce) package frozen raspberries

1 cup whipping cream

For the crust, in a medium bowl combine the graham cracker crumbs, sugar, cinnamon, and butter. Refrigerate ¹/₃ cup of the mixture. Press the remaining mixture into two 8 x 8-inch pans.

For the filling, in a large bowl beat the cream cheese until soft and fluffy. Add the confectioners' sugar, salt, and vanilla, mixing well. Spread over the crust.

For the topping, dissolve the gelatin in the boiling water. Add the lemon juice. Fold in the frozen raspberries. Stir until the raspberries are thawed and the mixture is partially thickened. Pour over the filling. In a medium bowl whip the cream. Spread over the raspberry layer, using a small spatula dipped in water. Sprinkle with the reserved crumbs. Chill until set, at least 4 hours.

Makes 10 to 12 servings

Judy Ross, Email Femail

Celtic Bells,
Baddeck, Nova Scotia

Grandma's Lemon Fluff

This is an old family recipe from my husband's grandmother, Florence.

1 (3-ounce) package lemon gelatin
1 1/2 cups hot water
  Juice of 1 large lemon
1 cup sugar

1 cup sweetened condensed milk, whipped and chilled
  Graham cracker crumbs

Dissolve the gelatin in hot water according to the package directions. Add the lemon juice and sugar. Whip with an electric mixer on medium speed. Mix in the sweetend condensed milk. Arrange a generous amount of graham cracker crumbs in the bottom of a 12 x 7-inch pan. Pour the mixture over the crumbs. Refrigerate for 8 hours or overnight.

Makes 8 to 10 servings

Sue Ellen Cooper, Exalted Queen Mother

*The Fabulous Founders,
Fullerton, California*

Peppermint Heaven

2 cups crushed chocolate sandwich cookies
1/2 gallon peppermint ice cream
1 jar hot fudge topping

1/2 cup chopped pecans
1 (8-ounce) carton frozen whipped topping, thawed

Press the cookie crumbs into a 13 x 9-inch pan. Place in the freezer while softening the ice cream. Spread the ice cream over the crumbs. Place in freezer until the ice cream hardens. Place the hot fudge topping in the microwave for 20 seconds, or until pourable. Spread over the ice cream. Sprinkle with the pecans. Place in the freezer until firm. Spread with the whipped topping and drizzle with additional hot fudge topping.

Makes 15 servings

Sharon Frisbie, Lady of the Net
Cardinal Hattitudes,
Campbell, Nebraska

Grasshopper Tarts

1/2 cup chocolate wafer crumbs	1 tablespoon crème de menthe
2 tablespoons butter, melted	1 tablespoon crème de cocoa
1 cup marshmallow crème	1/2 cup whipped cream

In a medium bowl combine the wafer crumbs and butter, stirring well. Press the crumb mixture into two 5-inch tart pans. In a medium bowl combine the marshmallow crème, crème de menthe, and crème de cocoa. Beat 1 minute on high speed with an electric mixer. Fold in the whipped cream. Pour over the crusts. Freeze.

Makes 4 servings

Charlotte Beasley, Queen Charlotte B.
So. Belles of Boca Raton,
Boca Raton, Florida

Irresistible Coconut Ice Cream Torte

18 macaroons, crushed	1 quart vanilla ice cream, softened
1/4 cup (1/2 stick) butter, melted	1 quart strawberry ice cream, softened
3/4 cup hot fudge topping	
26 snack-size Mounds candy bars	1/4 cup sliced almonds, toasted

In a small bowl combine the cookie crumbs and butter. Press into the bottom of a greased 10-inch springform pan. Freeze for 15 minutes.

In a microwave-safe bowl, heat the hot fudge topping on high in the microwave for 15 seconds, or until pourable. Spread over the crust. Arrange the candy bars around the edge of the pan standing on the ends. Freeze 15 minutes. Spread the vanilla ice cream over the hot fudge. Freeze 30 minutes.

Spread the strawberry ice cream over the vanilla layer. Sprinkle with the almonds. Cover and freeze until firm. The torte may be frozen up to 2 months. Remove from the freezer 10 minutes before serving. Remove the side of the pan and slice for serving.

Makes 12 to 14 servings

Susie Van Foeken, Queen

Hilmar Red Hat Readers,
Hilmar, California

A Medley of Other Sweet Pleasures

Puddings, trifles, soufflés—and assorted offerings

Like some of the more interesting people you know, these recipes are a little bit different—and very intriguing—but don't necessarily fit into some of the other dessert categories. What cook among us can resist a recipe like "Cinnamon Raisin Bread Pudding with Orange Butterscotch Sauce" or "Ricotta-Stuffed Blueberry Soufflé?" These recipes are ingenious and delectable!

Brownie Pudding

1 cup all-purpose flour	1 teaspoon vanilla
2 teaspoons baking powder	2 tablespoons melted butter
3/4 cup sugar	3/4 cup chopped nuts
1/2 teaspoon salt	3/4 cup firmly packed dark brown sugar
2 tablespoons plus 1/4 cup unsweetened cocoa powder, divided	1 1/4 cups very hot water
1/2 cup milk	Unsweetened whipped cream (optional)

Preheat the oven to 350 degrees.

In a large bowl combine the flour, baking powder, sugar, salt, and 2 tablespoons of the cocoa powder. Add the milk, vanilla, and butter. Mix until smooth. Add the nuts, mixing well. Pour into an 8 x 8-inch baking pan. In a small bowl mix the brown sugar and the remaining 1/4 cup cocoa powder and sprinkle evenly over the batter. Pour the hot water over the entire mixture. Do not stir. Bake 40 to 45 minutes. Cool on a wire rack. Serve warm with whipped cream, if desired.

Makes 6 to 8 servings

Carol Betush, Queen
Rebellious Elegant Dames,
Redding, California

Russian Cream with Raspberry Sauce

RUSSIAN CREAM:

1 (0.25-ounce) envelope unflavored gelatin
1/4 cup water
1/2 cup plus 2 tablespoons sugar
1 (3-ounce) package cream cheese, softened
1 cup whipping cream

1 cup sour cream
1 teaspoon vanilla

RASPBERRY SAUCE:

1 (10-ounce) package frozen raspberries
2 tablespoons raspberry liqueur

For the Russian cream, in a medium saucepan combine the gelatin and water. Let stand 1 minute. Add the sugar and stir over medium heat until dissolved. Cool.

In a large bowl beat the cream cheese. Add the whipping cream, sour cream, gelatin mixture, and vanilla. Beat until blended. Pour into parfait or other suitable serving dishes. Refrigerate until firm.

For the raspberry sauce, combine the raspberries, the remaining 2 tablespoons sugar, and the liqueur in a blender. Blend until smooth. Strain through a sieve to remove the raspberry seeds, if desired. Serve over the Russian cream.

Makes 4 servings

Beverly Carruthers, Queen Mother or Queen B

*Red Sails, London,
Ontario, Canada*

Cinnamon Raisin Bread Pudding with Orange Butterscotch Sauce

BREAD PUDDING:

2   tablespoons butter

2   apples, peeled and cubed

1/4   cup firmly packed light brown sugar

8   cups cubed raisin bread

6   large egg yolks

3   large eggs

1 1/2 cups granulated sugar

1   cup heavy cream

1   cup whole milk

1   tablespoon vanilla

1/2 tablespoon cinnamon

ORANGE BUTTERSCOTCH SAUCE:

2   tablespoons butter

1/4   cup firmly packed light brown sugar

1/4   cup orange liqueur

Juice of 1 orange

1/4   cup heavy cream

For the bread pudding, in a sauté pan melt the butter. Add the apples and brown sugar. Sauté until soft. Remove from the heat. Layer the bread cubes and the apple mixture in a 10 x 8-inch baking pan.

In a medium mixing bowl combine the eggs yolks, eggs, granulated sugar, heavy cream, milk, vanilla, and cinnamon. Beat well. Pour the mixture into the baking pan and let stand 15 minutes.

Preheat the oven to 350 degrees. Place the pan in a larger pan filled with water to within 1 inch of the top. Bake 35 minutes, or until a knife comes out clean. Allow to cool. Cut into squares.

For the sauce, in a small saucepan melt the butter. Add the brown sugar and allow the mixture to bubble. Add the orange liqueur and orange juice. Cook until the mixture has reduced by half. Add the heavy cream and reduce the mixture until lightly thickened. Serve with the bread pudding.

Makes 12 to 15 servings

Jo Martyn, Her Royal Highness of D'ssert

Nonpareils,
Knoxville, Tennessee

Heavenly Date Nut Pudding

1/2 cup (1 stick) butter, softened	11/2 teaspoons baking powder
1 cup sugar	1 cup pitted, chopped dates
2 large eggs, beaten	1 cup chopped walnuts or pecans
1 cup milk	Whipped cream, for garnish
11/2 tablespoons all-purpose flour	

Preheat the oven to 325 degrees. Grease a glass 8 x 8-inch baking pan.

In a large bowl cream the butter. Gradually add the sugar until light and fluffy. Add the eggs, milk, flour, and baking powder. Mix well. Fold in the dates and walnuts. Pour into the prepared baking dish. Bake 50 to 60 minutes, or until the pudding is set. Let cool. Serve with whipped cream.

Makes 6 to 8 servings

Judith Rumble, Queen

Rio Red Hots,
Rio Vista, California

Lemon Snow Pudding

PUDDING:

1 (0.25-ounce) envelope unflavored gelatin

1¼ cups water, divided

¾ cup sugar

⅛ teaspoon salt

¼ cup lemon juice

2 large egg whites

LEMON CUSTARD SAUCE:

½ cup heavy cream

2 large egg yolks

⅓ cup sugar

⅓ cup butter or margarine, melted

1 tablespoon grated lemon peel

2 tablespoons lemon juice

For the pudding, in a small saucepan, sprinkle the gelatin over ½ cup of the water. Let stand 2 minutes to soften. Place over low heat, stirring constantly, until the gelatin is dissolved. Stir in the sugar and salt. Remove from the heat and stir in the remaining ¾ cup water and the lemon juice. Refrigerate 1 hour, or until the consistency of unbeaten egg whites.

Using an electric mixer at high speed, add the egg whites and whip 20 minutes, or until stiff peaks form when the beater is slowly raised. Spoon into a 2-quart mold. Refrigerate overnight, or until well chilled and firm enough to unmold.

To serve run a small spatula around the edge of the mold. Invert over a serving platter. Place a hot, damp dishcloth on the bottom of the mold and shake gently to release.

For the sauce, beat the heavy cream in a small bowl until thick but not stiff. Set aside. In another small bowl, using the same beaters, beat the egg yolks until thick and lemon colored. Gradually add the sugar, and then gradually beat in the butter. Add the lemon peel and juice, beating well. Fold in the whipped cream. Refrigerate at least 2 hours or until well chilled.

Serve the sauce with the pudding.

Makes 8 servings

Merna Price, Queen Mother
Thousand Island Belles,
Gananoque, Ontario

Bailey's Chocolate Trifle

1 (18.25-ounce) package devil's food cake mix	3 1/2 cups cold whole milk
1 cup Irish cream liqueur	3 cups frozen whipped topping, thawed
2 (3.4-ounce) packages instant chocolate pudding mix	

Preheat the oven to 350 degrees.

Prepare the cake according to the package directions. Bake in a greased 13 x 9-inch pan. Cool 1 hour on a wire rack. Poke holes in the cake about 2 inches apart with a meat fork. Carefully pour the Irish cream over the cake. Refrigerate 1 hour.

In a medium bowl whisk the pudding mix and milk together until smooth. Let stand 2 or 3 minutes, or until soft set. Cut the cake into 1 1/2-inch cubes. Place one-third of the cubes in a trifle bowl. Top with one-third of the pudding and one-third of the whipped topping. Repeat the layers 2 times. Store in the refrigerator until ready to serve.

Makes 14 to 16 servings

Joanne Burt, Duchess Desert Cat
Desert Darlins,
Sun City, Arizona

Chocolate Chile Bread Pudding

6 tablespoons butter	3/4 teaspoon cayenne
12 ounces fine-quality bittersweet chocolate	2 cups heavy cream
2 tablespoons sugar	6 large eggs, lightly beaten
1 tablespoon vanilla	12 slices firm white sandwich bread, cut into small cubes
1 1/2 teaspoons cinnamon	

Place the oven rack in the middle position and preheat the oven to 350 degrees. Generously butter a 13 x 9-inch baking pan. Set aside.

In top of a double boiler melt the butter and chocolate over simmering water. Stir in the sugar, vanilla, cinnamon, and cayenne. Remove the pan from the heat. Pour the mixture into a large mixing bowl. Whisk in the heavy cream. Whisk in the eggs. Fold in the bread cubes, and let stand at least 5 minutes. Fill the prepared pan with the bread mixture. Bake 15 to 25 minutes, or until puffed and set around the edges but still moist in the center. Cool 5 minutes before serving. Serve with vanilla ice cream, if desired.

Makes 10 to 12 servings

Gloria Wade, Queen Mother

Mad Red Hatters,
Hendersonville, Tennessee

Pumpkin Cobbler

3 large eggs, beaten
1 (15-ounce) can pumpkin
1 (12-ounce) can evaporated milk
1 cup sugar
1/8 teaspoon salt
1 1/2 teaspoons cinnamon

1 teaspoon ground ginger
1 tablespoon vanilla extract
1 (18.25-ounce) package yellow cake mix
1 1/4 cups (2 1/2 sticks) butter, melted
1 cup chopped nuts

Preheat the oven to 350 degrees.

In a large bowl combine the eggs, pumpkin, evaporated milk, sugar, salt, cinnamon, ginger, and vanilla, mixing well. Pour into an ungreased 13 x 9-inch baking pan. Sprinkle the cake mix over the top. Drizzle with the melted butter. Bake 25 minutes. Top with the nuts. Bake an additional 15 minutes.

Makes 8 to 10 servings

Bonnie Zarch, Queen Mother
Red Hot Red Hats Too,
Skokie, Illinois

Mom's Rhubarb Custard Dessert

CRUST:

1 1/2 cups all-purpose flour

3/4 cup (1 1/2 sticks) butter or margarine

1 tablespoon sugar

FILLING:

1 1/2 cups sugar

2 tablespoons cornstarch

3 cups fresh rhubarb, cut into 1/2-inch pieces, or 1 (20-ounce) package frozen rhubarb

1/2 cup milk or light cream

1/3 cup orange juice

3 large egg yolks, lightly beaten

MERINGUE:

3 large egg whites

3 tablespoons sugar

1 teaspoon vanilla extract

Preheat the oven to 375 degrees.

For the crust, in a large bowl combine the flour, butter, and sugar, mixing until crumbly. Press the flour mixture into an ungreased 13 x 9-inch pan. Bake 15 to 20 minutes, or until golden brown. While the crust is baking, prepare the filling and the meringue.

For the filling, in a medium saucepan, combine the sugar and cornstarch, stirring to mix. Add the rhubarb, milk, and orange juice. Cook over medium heat until the rhubarb is tender and the mixture is thickened, stirring constantly. Remove from the heat. Stir a small amount of the hot mixture into the egg yolks. Add the egg yolks to the cooked rhubarb. Return to the heat and bring to a boil. Set aside to cool.

For the meringue, in a small bowl beat the egg whites until frothy. Gradually add the sugar, beating constantly until stiff peaks form. Blend in the vanilla and set aside. Remove the baked crust from the oven and reduce the temperature to 350 degrees. Pour the slightly cooled filling over the crust. Spoon the meringue over the filling, spreading to cover and sealing to edges. Bake 12 to 15 minutes, or until the meringue is golden brown. Cool before serving. Store in the refrigerator.

Makes 12 to 15 servings

June Goplin DeWerff, Queen

Sizzling Scarlet Sisters,
Moorhead, Minnesota

From L to R: *Glorian Venturella and JoAnn Porrello dancing.*

Photo submitted by JoAnn Porrello, Go for It Gals, Oakland Gardens, New York.

Angel Cream Melba

3 (0.25-ounce) envelopes unflavored gelatin	4 cups heavy whipping cream
1 cup sugar	1 (10-ounce) package frozen raspberries, thawed
3/4 teaspoon salt	2 teaspoons cornstarch
4 cups milk, divided	1 (10-ounce) package frozen peaches, thawed
4 teaspoons vanilla extract	

In a 2-quart saucepan combine the gelatin, sugar, and salt. Gradually stir in 2 cups of the milk. Cook over medium heat, stirring frequently, until the gelatin is completely dissolved. Remove from the heat. Stir in the vanilla and the remaining 2 cups milk. Refrigerate 30 minutes, or until the mixture mounds slightly when dropped from a spoon.

In a large bowl with the mixer at medium speed, beat the cream until soft peaks form. Using a wire whisk, gently fold the gelatin mixture into the whipped cream. Pour the mixture into a 12-cup ring mold or Bundt pan. Refrigerate at least 3 hours or overnight until set.

Mash the raspberries. Combine the raspberries and cornstarch in a 1-quart saucepan. Cook over medium heat until the mixture boils, stirring constantly. Stir in the peaches with their syrup until blended. Refrigerate the sauce until well chilled.

To serve, unmold the Angel Cream onto a chilled platter. Cut into slices and serve on dessert plates. Spoon the sauce over each serving and pass the remaining sauce.

Makes 24 servings

Judith A. Yanarelli, Filly of Finance
Dizzy Dames of Unknown Fame,
Clifton, New Jersey

Pineapple–Cherry Bisque Dessert

1 (12-ounce) package vanilla wafers, ground finely

1 cup sugar

1/4 cup (1/2 stick) margarine, melted

4 large eggs whites

1 cup (2 sticks) margarine, softened

4 cups confectioners' sugar

1 (20-ounce) can crushed pineapple, well drained

1 (8-ounce) jar maraschino cherries, sliced in half

1 cup chopped walnuts or pecans

1 pint heavy whipping cream

In a medium bowl combine the cookie crumbs, sugar, and the melted margarine. Stir until well blended. Press the mixture firmly into the bottom of a well-greased 13 x 9-inch pan.

In a large bowl beat the egg whites until very stiff. In another bowl cream the softened margarine and confectioners' sugar until totally blended. Gently fold the beaten egg whites into the creamed mixture. Spread evenly over the crust. Sprinkle the crushed pineapple over the creamed layer. Set aside 20 cherry halves as a garnish. Sprinkle with the remaining cherry halves. Sprinkle the nuts over the pineapple and cherries.

In a medium bowl whip the heavy cream until thick. Evenly spread the whipped cream over the entire mixture. Garnish with the reserved cherry halves. Refrigerate 10 to 12 hours or overnight before serving.

Makes 20 servings

Stephanie Siebert, Lady Stephanie
Red Hat Rebels,
Las Vegas, Nevada

Ricotta-Stuffed Blueberry Soufflé

2 large eggs	Cooking spray
1/2 cup heavy cream	1/3 cup whole-milk ricotta cheese
1/3 cup seltzer water	Few drops orange oil or zest
1 teaspoon vanilla	1 cup fresh or frozen blueberries
1/3 cup plus 2 tablespoons plus 1/4 cup sugar or artificial sweetener, divided	1/4 cup plus 2 tablespoons water, divided
1/2 cup soy flour	1 teaspoon cornstarch
2 tablespoons oat flour	Pinch of cinnamon and nutmeg
1 tablespoon vital wheat gluten	
1/4 teaspoon orange oil or orange zest (optional)	

Preheat the oven to 400 degrees.

In a blender combine the eggs, heavy cream, seltzer water, vanilla, 1/3 cup of the sugar, soy flour, oat flour, wheat gluten, and orange oil, if desired. Blend well. Divide evenly into four ramekins or large custard cups sprayed with cooking spray. Place the ramekins in a 13 x 9-inch pan and add boiling water to the depth of 1 inch.

In a small bowl mix the ricotta cheese, 2 tablespoons of the sugar, and a few drops of orange oil. Drop evenly into the centers of each ramekin. Slightly spoon the batter over the dollops of cheese without disturbing them. Bake for 18 to 20 minutes, or until golden brown.

Meanwhile, in a small saucepan simmer the blueberries, 2 tablespoons of the water, and the remaining ¼ cup sugar over medium-low heat. Combine the cornstarch with the remaining ¼ cup water, mixing well. Stir into the blueberries. Add the cinnamon and nutmeg. Stir constantly until the liquid is clear. Remove from the heat.

When ready to serve, remove the soufflés from the ramekins and top with the blueberry sauce. Leave any unused portions in the ramekins and top with the sauce. Cover with plastic wrap and refrigerate until ready to serve.

Makes 4 servings

Nancy Bailey, Not-So-Dumb-Blondie

Sexy Sadies,
Mesa, Arizona

At our very first "Red Hat Birthday Party," we all celebrated by wearing our reverse colors. We even played with bubbles and wore big red waxed lips—don't we look great?!

L to R: *Lynn Turnbull, Joyce Passavant, Tracey Cwirko, and Elaine Gundy.*

Photo submitted by Joyce Passavant, The Ruby Divine Divas, Hamburg, New Jersey.

Caramel Custard

1½ cups sugar, divided		2	teaspoons vanilla extract
6	large eggs	3	cups milk

In a heavy saucepan over low heat, cook ¾ cup of the sugar until melted and golden, stirring constantly. Pour into eight 6-ounce custard cups, tilting to cover the bottom of each cup. Let stand 10 minutes.

Preheat the oven to 350 degrees.

In a large bowl beat the eggs, vanilla, milk, and the remaining ¾ cup sugar until combined but not foamy. Pour over the caramelized sugar.

Place the custard cups in two 8 x 8-inch baking pans. Pour boiling water into the pans to a depth of 1 inch. Bake 40 to 45 minutes, or until a knife inserted near the center comes out clean. Remove the cups from the pans and cool on wire racks.

To unmold, run a knife around the rim of each cup and invert onto a dessert plate. Serve warm or chilled.

Makes 8 servings

Mary Louise Stagner, Queen Gadabout
Cardinal Red Hats,
Poplar Bluff, Missouri

Cream Puff Dessert

1 cup water	2 (3.4-ounce) packages instant chocolate pudding
1/2 cup (1 stick) butter	
1 cup all-purpose flour	1 (8-ounce) container frozen whipped topping, thawed
4 large eggs	
1 (8-ounce) package cream cheese, softened	1/4 cup chocolate ice cream topping
	1/4 cup caramel ice cream topping
31/2 cups cold milk	1/3 cup toasted sliced almonds

Preheat the oven to 400 degrees. Grease a 13 x 9-inch baking pan.

In a large saucepan over medium heat bring the water and butter to a boil. Add the flour, stirring until a smooth ball forms. Remove from the heat. Let stand 5 minutes. Add the eggs, one at a time, beating well with a wooden spoon after each addition. Beat until smooth and a ball forms again. Spread into the prepared pan, allowing some of the dough to spread 1/4 inch up the sides of the pan. Bake 30 to 35 minutes, or until puffed and golden brown. Cool completely on a wire rack.

In a medium bowl beat the cream cheese, milk, and pudding mix until smooth. Spread over the baked puff. Refrigerate 20 minutes.

Spread with the whipped topping. Drizzle with the chocolate and caramel toppings. Sprinkle with the toasted almonds. Keep refrigerated until ready to serve.

Makes 12 servings

Mary Petruniak, Traveling Mary
Red Bonnet Sisiters,
Lakeland, Florida

Lemon Lush

1 cup all-purpose flour
1 cup finely chopped walnuts
1/2 cup (1 stick) butter
1 (8-ounce) package cream cheese, softened
1 (16-ounce) container frozen whipped topping, thawed and divided

1 cup confectioners' sugar
2 (3.4-ounce) packages instant lemon pudding
2 tablespoons lemon zest
1/3 cup chopped walnuts, for garnish

Preheat the oven to 375 degrees.

In a small bowl combine the flour and walnuts. Cut in the butter with a pastry cutter. Press into a 13 x 9-inch baking pan. Bake 15 minutes. Cool on a wire rack 15 minutes. In a medium bowl blend the cream cheese, half the whipped topping, and the confectioners' sugar. Spread over the crust and chill 15 minutes. Prepare the lemon pudding as directed on the package. Add the lemon zest. When the pudding is set, spread over the cream cheese mixture. Chill 15 minutes. Spread with the rest of the whipped topping. Sprinkle the walnuts on top. Chill until ready to serve.

Makes 12 servings

Elaine Strong, Queen Elaine

Diamond Divas of Sonora,
Sahuarita, Arizona

Middle Eastern Orange Dessert

4 large oranges	1 tablespoon butter
1/2 cup plus 2 tablespoons hot water	1 teaspoon salt
1/3 to 1/2 cup honey	1 (3-ounce) package cream cheese, softened
1 teaspoon rose water	
1 cup chopped, almonds	1/2 cup heavy cream

Using a vegetable peeler, carefully remove the peel from 1 orange. Cut into 2-inch strips and cook in a saucepan with the hot water. Add the honey and rose water, and cook slowly until the orange peel is translucent. Remove from the stove.

Peel the oranges and remove all the white pith. Slice the oranges thin, removing any seeds. Heat the slices in the cooked peel and syrup for 3 minutes. Cool and place the orange slices and syrup in 6 serving dishes.

Preheat the oven to 400 degrees. In a small oven-safe bowl combine the almonds, butter, and salt. Place on a baking sheet and brown 15 minutes, stirring occasionally. Remove from the oven and set aside.

In a medium bowl combine the cream cheese and heavy cream. Beat until smooth. Spoon the sauce over the orange slices. Sprinkle with the toasted almonds. Serve warm.

Makes 6 servings

Darlene Schlemmer, Princess Dar

Red Rovers,
Kent, Ohio

Brittles, Truffles and Assorted Candies

Crunchy, chewy, or melt-in-your-mouth confections

The texture of our food provides part of the experience of eating. Flavor is important, of course, but no more so than the crunch of peanuts or the velvety smoothness of buttercream against the tongue. Mmmmmmmm! There have been personality quizzes purporting to describe people by analyzing their food preferences. Some claim that those who prefer crunchy foods are more assertive and vigorous, while those who love creamy smooth things are more sensual. But what if you absolutely love both? Does that mean you have a split personality—or just that you love dessert?

Aloha Brittle

1/2 cup sweetened flaked coconut	1 teaspoon butter
1 cup sugar	1 teaspoon baking soda
1/2 cup light corn syrup	1 teaspoon water
1 (3 1/4-ounce) jar macadamia nuts	2 teaspoons vanilla extract
1/2 cup chopped pecans	

On a greased baking pan, sprinkle the coconut in a 12-inch circle.

In a heavy saucepan combine the sugar and corn syrup. Cook over medium heat, stirring constantly until a candy thermometer reads 240 degrees (soft-ball stage). Stir in the macadamia nuts, pecans, and butter. Cook and stir until the mixture reaches 300 degrees (hard-crack stage).

In a small measuring cup, stir together the baking soda, water, and vanilla. Remove the saucepan from the heat. Stir in the baking soda mixture. Pour quickly over the coconut. Cool for 30 minutes. Lift the edges to loosen and then break into pieces. Store in an airtight container with waxed paper between layers.

Makes 1 pound

Sarah Hardimon, The Creative Gourmet

Elegant Swans,
Winter Park, Florida

Apricot Truffles

1/2 cup heavy whipping cream	1/3 cup chopped dried apricots
2 pounds of white chocolate, divided	Confectioners' sugar
25 drops apricot flavoring	

Heat the cream in the top of a double boiler over simmering water. Add 1 pound of the white chocolate. Let the mixture stand for about 10 minutes, and then mix well. Add the apricot flavoring and dried apricots, mixing well.

Pour the hot mixture (ganache) into a container with a tight-fitting lid. Refrigerate 24 hours. When ready to mold the truffles, remove from the refrigerator and let stand at room temperature for at least 4 hours.

Using a teaspoon, scrape across the ganache 3 to 4 times. Lightly powder your hands with confectioners' sugar, and then roll the mixture into a ball. Set the truffle onto waxed paper. Repeat using the remaining mixture.

In the top of a double boiler over boiling water, melt the remaining 1 pound white chocolate. Pour into a bowl. Dip the truffles into the melted chocolate. (You can use a dipping tool found at your local craft store or a fork.) Tap the side of the bowl to allow the excess chocolate to drip off. Place the rolled truffles onto a baking sheet covered with waxed paper. Allow the truffles to dry. Store in an airtight container. Rolled truffles will last in a cool, dark, dry place for up to 5 weeks, and the ganache will keep in the refrigerator up to 2 months in an airtight container.

Makes 30 truffles

Joann Heisch, Truffle Queen
Rovin' Rubies,
Auburn, California

Microwave Peanut Brittle

1 cup sugar	1 tablespoon butter
1/2 cup lily white corn syrup	1 teaspoon vanilla
1 1/2 cups salted peanuts	1 teaspoon baking soda

Coat a 1 1/2-quart microwave-safe dish with cooking spray. Add the sugar and corn syrup. Microwave on high for 3 minutes 40 seconds. Stir in the peanuts. Microwave on high for 3 minutes 30 seconds. Add the butter and the vanilla. Stir and microwave on high for 1 minute 40 seconds. Add the baking soda, and stir until foamy. Quickly pour and spread the mixture onto a well-greased cookie sheet. Cool and break into pieces.

Makes 1 pound

Elaine Ingersoll, Lady Las Vegas
Cold Lake Jet Setters,
Cold Lake, Alberta

Easy Pralines

1/2 cup firmly packed light brown sugar	1/4 cup butter or margarine
1 1/2 cups granulated sugar	1 teaspoon vanilla
8 tablespoons water	2 cups chopped pecans

In a medium saucepan boil the sugars and water for 3 minutes. Remove from the heat and add the butter. Add the vanilla and pecans. Stir quickly. Quickly drop onto waxed paper coated with cooking spray because they start to harden fast.

Makes 2 dozen

Sharon Hutchison, Scrapbooker
Racy Reds,
Kaufman, TX

Easy Chocolate Truffles

3 ounces unsweetened chocolate	3 large egg yolks
1 1/4 cups confectioners' sugar	1 teaspoon vanilla
1/3 cup butter or margarine, softened	Chocolate sprinkles

In the top of a double boiler over boiling water, melt the chocolate. In a medium bowl cream the confectioners' sugar and butter together. Add the egg yolks, one at a time, mixing well after each addition. Stir in the melted chocolate and the vanilla. Chill until the mixture is cool enough to handle.

Shape the mixture into small balls and roll in the chocolate sprinkles. Place on a baking sheet and let set for 1 hour. Store in the refrigerator. The truffles will keep approximately 1 week.

Makes 4 to 6 servings

Wini Hamilton, Queen Bitchyboss
Cackling Crows,
Woodbridge, Virginia

Cracker Brittle Crunch

1	sleeve saltine crackers	1/4	teaspoon baking soda
1	cup (2 sticks) butter		Walnuts, pecans, or chocolate chips (optional)
1	cup firmly packed dark brown sugar		

Preheat the oven to 350 degrees. Line a baking pan with aluminum foil. Spray lightly with cooking spray. Lay the crackers in rows to cover the entire pan.

In a small saucepan melt the butter and brown sugar. Bring to a boil, stirring constantly, for 3 minutes. Remove from the heat and add the baking soda, stirring well. Pour the mixture over the crackers and bake 6 to 8 minutes. (The crackers will look like they are floating in bubbles.) Remove and top with nuts or chocolate chips, if desired. Cool in the refrigerator until set. Break into pieces and store in airtight containers in the refrigerator.

Makes about 1 pound

Mary Jane MacVicar, Queen
Scarlett Shady Ladies,
Leamington, Ontario

Tipsy Truffles

1 1/2 cups sugar

1 cup water

1 1/2 cups nuts, finely chopped

1 1/2 cups crushed shortbread

4 pieces unsweetened chocolate

2 large egg yolks

2 tablespoons unsweetened cocoa powder

10 teaspoons sweet unsalted butter

2 tablespoons almond liqueur

Almond liqueur

Chocolate sprinkles or finely chopped nuts

In a medium saucepan bring the sugar and water to a boil, stirring constantly. Add the nuts, shortbread, unsweetened chocolate, egg yolks, cocoa powder, butter, and 2 tablespoons almond liqueur. Stir the mixture over low heat until well blended. Cool completely. Moisten hands with almond liqueur and form the mixture into 1-inch balls. Roll in either chocolate sprinkles or chopped nuts.

Makes 50 truffles

Bessie Barnes, Queen
Literary Ladies,
Virginia Beach, Virginia

Buckeye Balls Candy

This is an Ohio favorite.

---

1 1/2 cups peanut butter
1/2 cup (1 stick) butter, softened
2 cups confectioners' sugar

1 teaspoon vanilla
2 tablespoons vegetable oil
1 (6-ounce) package semisweet chocolate chips

In a large bowl beat the peanut butter and butter. Add the confectioners' sugar and vanilla. Mix well. Roll into balls and place on waxed paper-lined cookie sheets. Refrigerate until chilled.

In a microwave-safe bowl combine the oil and chocolate chips. Microwave on high for 1 minute, or until the chocolate is melted. Using a toothpick, dip half of each peanut butter ball into the melted chocolate. Return to the cookie sheet and refrigerate until ready to serve.

Makes about 2 dozen

Joanne Augenstein, Queen of Mirth and Merriment

Red Birds of a Feather,
Yellow Springs, Ohio

Coconut Balls

3 cups finely shredded sweetened coconut

3 cups confectioners' sugar

1/2 cup hot mashed potatoes

1/4 cake paraffin wax

1 pound semisweet chocolate chips

In a large bowl blend the coconut and confectioners' sugar. Add the hot mashed potatoes, blending well with a fork. Shape the mixture into balls and place on waxed paper.

In a heavy saucepan melt the paraffin wax and chocolate chips. Insert a toothpick into each ball and dip into the melted chocolate until well coated. Place on waxed paper and cool until firm. Store in the refrigerator.

Makes 2 dozen

Jody Hogan , Queen of Fine Threads

The Ram,
Cow Bay, Nova Scotia

Date Smash

2 cups sugar

1/2 cup milk

1 cup chopped dates

1 cup chopped nuts

1 teaspoon vanilla

In a medium saucepan combine the sugar and milk. Cook over medium heat, stirring constantly, until a digital candy thermometer reads 240 degrees (soft-ball stage). Add the dates, nuts, and vanilla. Beat until creamy and thick. Pour into a greased 8 x 8-inch pan or a pie pan. Cut into squares to serve.

Makes 3 dozen

Janice Maupin, Royal Jester
Crimson & Clover,
Topeka, Kansas

Potato Candy

1	small or medium boiled potato		Confectioners' sugar
1½	teaspoons vanilla	1	cup peanut butter
1	(1-pound) package confectioners' sugar		

In a medium bowl mash the potato. Add the vanilla. Mix the pound of confectioners' sugar with the mashed potato until combined enough to roll out. Sprinkle additional confectioners' sugar on a table or board. Roll out the potato mixture. Spread with the peanut butter, and then roll up jelly-roll fashion. Wrap in plastic wrap, chill, and then cut into slices. Store in an airtight container.

Makes 30 candies

Brenda Hansen, Queen
Red Hat Sun Dolls,
Youngtown, Arizona

Kentucky Bourbon Balls

½ cup bourbon
1 cup chopped pecans
1 pound confectioners' sugar
(1 stick) butter

1 (12-ounce) package unsweetened chocolate chips
1 cake paraffin

In a bowl, pour the bourbon over the pecans and let stand 1 hour or overnight if possible. In a large bowl cream together the confectioners' sugar and butter. Stir in the nut and whiskey mixture. Place in the freezer or refrigerator until firm enough to shape into 1-inch balls. Shape using a 1-inch ice cream scoop with a spring-loaded handle. Place the shaped balls in the freezer on lined cookie sheets until hard enough to dip.

In the top of a double boiler over boiling water, melt the chocolate and paraffin (or melt in the microwave in a microwave-safe container). Using a fork or toothpick, dip one ball at a time in the chocolate. Place on waxed paper-lined cookie sheets. Chill again. These keep best in sealed containers in the refrigerator until ready to serve.

Makes about 32 candies

Rosa Floyd, Regal Rosa
Blue Grass Red Hat Society,
Lexington, Kentucky

Peanut Butter Fudge

2 cups firmly packed light brown sugar	1/2 teaspoon salt
2 cups granulated sugar	2 cups marshmallow crème
3/4 cup whole milk	2 cups chunky peanut butter
	1 teaspoon vanilla

In a large saucepan mix the sugars and milk. Bring the mixture to a boil over medium heat. Boil, stirring constantly, for about 5 minutes, or until the temperature reaches between 234 and 240 degrees on a candy thermometer.

Remove from the heat and add the salt, marshmallow crème, peanut butter, and vanilla. Mix briskly and thoroughly. Line a 13 x 9-inch pan with buttered foil that overlaps the edges of the pan. Pour in the fudge. Cool and then remove the foil to cut the fudge into squares.

Makes 8 to 9 dozen

Mary McGee, Queenie
Scarlet Women of Portsmouth,
Portsmouth, New Hampshire

Fleming Fudge

1 (18-ounce) package chocolate chips	1 cup chopped pecans or walnuts
1 (12-ounce) can evaporated milk	Pinch of salt
	1 1/2 teaspoons vanilla

Grease a 13 x 9-inch glass baking dish. Set aside.

In a medium saucepan combine the chocolate chips and evaporated milk. Cook over low heat until the chips melt. Remove from heat. Add the nuts, salt, and vanilla. Spoon evenly into the prepared baking dish. Refrigerate for at least 2 hours. Cut into squares.

Makes 2 dozen pieces

Barb Bailey, Member
Red Hatted Stepchild,
Ocean Springs, Mississippi

Chocolate Peanut Clusters

8 squares white almond bark
1 (1.5-ounce) package milk
   chocolate chips

1 1/2 (16-ounce) cans cocktail peanuts
   or mixed nuts

In a microwave-safe bowl, microwave the almond bark 1 minute. Stir and microwave 1 minute longer. Remove from the microwave and stir. Top with the chocolate chips, but do not stir. Microwave for 2 minutes. Remove from the microwave and stir until the chocolate is melted. Stir in the peanuts. Drop by teaspoonful onto waxed paper and let stand 30 minutes, or until set. Store in an airtight container or freeze in freezer bags.

Makes 2 dozen

BJ Birmingham, Queen Snowflake
Red Hat Tamales,
Bartlesville, Oklahoma

Red Hat Easy Chocolate Fudge

1 (16-ounce) package confectioners' sugar	1/4 cup evaporated milk
1/2 cup unsweetened cocoa powder	1 teaspoon vanilla
1/2 cup (1 stick) butter or margarine	3/4 cup chopped walnuts or pecans (optional)

In a microwave-safe bowl mix the confectioners' sugar and cocoa powder. Add the butter and evaporated milk. Cover the bowl and microwave on high for 2 minutes. Remove from the microwave and stir well. Cover again and microwave for 2 more minutes. Remove from the microwave and add the vanilla and chopped nuts, if desired. Pour into a greased 8 x 8-inch pan and refrigerate for 2 hours or longer before cutting.

Makes 2 dozen

Lois Dill, Chapterette
River Red Hatters,
DeBary, Florida

Best Maple Walnut Fudge Ever

1 1/2 cups firmly packed dark brown sugar	Pinch of salt
1/2 cup (1 stick) butter	1/2 teaspoon vanilla
1/2 cup evaporated milk	2 cups confectioners' sugar
	1/2 cup chopped walnuts

In a medium saucepan combine the brown sugar and butter. Bring to a boil. Remove from the stove and stir in the evaporated milk. Return the pan to the stove. Cook, stirring constantly, for 4 minutes over medium-high heat. Remove from the heat. Add the salt, vanilla, confectioners' sugar, and walnuts. Stir well. Pour the mixture into a buttered 8 x 8-inch pan. Cool and cut into squares.

Makes 2 dozen pieces

Shirley Murphy, Lady Smurf
Red Hat Divas Toronto,
Toronto, Ontario

Great-Grandmom's Buttercream Easter Eggs

1 cup (2 sticks) butter or margarine	Milk, if needed
2 (1-pound) packages confectioners' sugar	8 ounces Baker's semisweet chocolate
1 large egg white	2 tablespoons paraffin wax (optional)
1 teaspoon vanilla	

In a large bowl cream the butter. Add the confectioners' sugar gradually. Add the egg white and vanilla. Add a small amount of milk if the mixture is dry. Shape into eggs and put on waxed paper. Let stand 3 hours. Melt the chocolate and paraffin wax, if using. Dip the eggs in the melted chocolate.

Makes 10 chocolate eggs

Mary Jean O'Keefe, Creative Countess
Parkville Scarlet O'Hattas,
Baltimore, Maryland

Total Joys

6   Almond Joy candy bars

1   (13-ounce) jar marshmallow crème

6   to 8 cups Total cereal

Butter or margarine

Nuts, candied fruit, or rice cereal (if desired)

In the top of a double boiler over boiling water, melt the candy bars and marshmallow crème until smooth. Stir in the cereal. While the mixture is still hot, butter an 8 x 8 baking pan and your hands. Press the mixture into the baking pan, making sure all of the corners are full. Cool in the refrigerator 3 hours, or until hardened. When cool, cut into 1-inch squares.

Makes 2 dozen

Beth Best, Countess BusyBee

Vintage Roses,
Collegedale, Tennessee

Caramel Pretzel Candies

1   (12-ounce) package soft caramels   1   (12-ounce) bag pecan halves
1   (16-ounce) bag mini pretzels

Preheat the oven to 250 degrees. Place as many pretzels on a baking sheet that will fit. Place a caramel on top of each pretzel. Bake 8 to 10 minutes to slightly soften the caramel. Immediately after removing the pretzels from the cookie sheet, place a pecan half on top of each caramel, pressing down slightly to stick to the pretzel. Chill in the refrigerator. Store in a covered container.

Note: You will have pretzels and pecans left over for making other recipes.

Makes about 3 dozen

Ernette Douglas, Queen Mother
Ladies Of Leisure,
Jacksonville, Florida

White Chocolate Macadamia Nut Bars

2 cups semisweet chocolate chips, divided

2 cups white chocolate chips, divided

2/3 cup toasted macadamia nuts, coarsely chopped

Line a 13 x 9-inch cookie sheet with parchment paper with 2 inches hanging over the sides of the cookie sheet.

Set aside 1/4 cup chocolate chips. In a microwave-safe dish, microwave the remaining 13/4 cups chocolate chips on medium for 2 minutes, stirring every 30 seconds, or until smooth. Pour the melted chocolate over the prepared cookie sheet. Spread to form an even layer.

Set aside 1/4 cup of the white chocolate chips. Melt the remaining 13/4 cups white chocolate chips on Medium for 2 minutes, stirring every 30 seconds, until smooth. Pour the melted white chocolate over the dark chocolate. Swirl with a toothpick or skewer to create a marble effect. Sprinkle the nuts on top. Press the nuts and the reserved semisweet and white chocolate chips into the melted chocolate. Refrigerate for 30 minutes, or place in the freezer for 10 to 15 minutes, or until firm. Remove from the paper and cut or break into bite-size pieces.

Makes 3 to 4 dozen

Charlene Shipman, Queen Char

Glitzy Chicks,
Auburn, Washington

Thirst-Satisfying Beverages

Hot or cold, spiked or straight-laced

So . . . desserts can be cakes, pies, puddings, cookies, bars, candies . . . ad infinitum. But what about *drinking* your dessert? It is possible to do, as the following recipes prove. It is also possible (and a bit over-the-top) to enjoy one of these drinks along *with* a piece of cake or a slice of pie—which, of course, you whipped up using this book. Then you can have dessert with your dessert. Remember what Mae West said, "Too much of a good thing is wonderful."

Lavender Breakfast Punch

2 cups water

2/3 cup sugar

1 (3-inch) mesh tea infuser filled half full with dried lavender blossoms

3 tablespoons snipped fresh mint or 1 1/2 tablespoons dried mint

1 cup orange juice

1/2 cup lemon juice

2 cups strong brewed tea

1 (1-liter) bottle 7-Up, chilled

In a large stainless-steel pan, combine the water and sugar. Bring to a boil over medium heat. Remove the pan from the heat and place the mesh tea infuser and the mint into the pan. Steep for 20 minutes. Add the orange juice, lemon juice, and brewed tea to the flavored lavender water. Chill. Just before serving, add the 7-Up.

Note: Lavender can be found in bulk at health food stores.

Makes 3 quarts

Sheri Nelson, Princess Quite-a-Lot of Shoes, and Julie Morrow, Princess Amidala Rose

Titian Queens and Ladies-In-Waiting, Helena, Montana

Slush Punch

2 1/2 cups sugar

  6 cups water

  2 (3-ounce) packages strawberry
      gelatin

  1 (46-ounce) can pineapple juice

2/3 cup lemon juice

  1 quart orange juice

  2 (2-liter) bottles lemon-lime soda,
      divided

In a large saucepan, combine the sugar, water, and gelatin. Boil for 3 minutes. Stir in the pineapple juice, lemon juice, and orange juice. Divide the mixture in half and freeze in two separate containers.

When ready to serve, place the frozen contents of one container in a punch bowl. Stir in 1 of the bottles of the lemon-lime soda until slushy. Refill the punch bowl with the remaining frozen slush and the remaining soda when needed.

Makes 50 servings

Janet Amon, Queen Mother

Sass With Class,
Largo, Florida

Holiday Punch

1	quart cranberry juice	1/4	cup freshly squeezed lemon juice
1	cup sugar	2	cups chilled ginger ale
2	cups orange juice	1	cup vodka or gin
1	cup pineapple juice	1	quart rainbow sherbet

In a large container, combine the cranberry juice, sugar, orange juice, pineapple juice, and lemon juice. Cover and refrigerate. To serve, pour the juices into a punch bowl. Stir in the ginger ale and vodka or gin. Float scoops of the sherbet on top.

Makes about 20 servings

Carolyn Hardimon, The Recipe Lady
Elegant Swans ,
Belleville, Illinois

To-Die-For Wedding Punch

1 (12-ounce) can frozen orange juice, thawed

1 (12-ounce) can frozen pink lemonade, thawed

2 (6-ounce) cans frozen strawberry daiquiri mix, thawed

2 1/2 cups water

2 cups peach or apricot nectar

1 cup peach schnapps (optional)

4 (12-ounce) cans lemon-lime soda, chilled

1 quart raspberry sherbet, softened or 6 medium strawberries, sliced

1 large ice ring (frozen the day before)

In a punch bowl combine the orange juice, lemonade, and daiquiri mix. Stir in the water, nectar, and schnapps, if desired. Chill.

To serve, add the soda and sherbet. Stir together and add the ice ring in center.

Note: To make the ice ring, place water in a Bundt pan. Stir in a few drops of food coloring and freeze overnight.

Makes 32 to 35 servings

Lynda Herzog Pope, Queen Mother of All
Herzog's Hilarious Hellyun Hairdressers & Healthcare Heiffers of Haughton
Haughton, Louisiana

Wonderful Winter Tea

6 tea bags	1 (6-ounce) can frozen orange juice
14 cups water, divided	1 (6-ounce) can frozen lemonade
1 1/2 cups sugar	1 tablespoon ground cinnamon

In a large saucepan combine the tea bags and 4 cups of the water. Bring to a boil. Remove from the heat and steep for 15 to 20 minutes. Remove the tea bags.

In a 1 gallon pitcher, combine the tea, sugar, frozen juices, cinnamon, and the remaining 10 cups water. Mix well.

The tea can be served warm, at room temperature, or over ice. Leftovers can be stored in the refrigerator for up to two weeks.

Makes 20 servings

Carol Goldman, HRM (Her Royal Mess) Dutchess of Faux

Brandon's Bodacious Bades,
Florence, Mississippi

Strawberry Slush

9 cups water

2 cups vodka

2 cups sugar

1 (12-ounce) can frozen orange juice

2 small envelopes unsweetened strawberry Kool-Aid

2 (12-ounce) packages frozen strawberries

Lemon-lime soda, ginger ale, or Champagne

In a large saucepan combine the water, vodka, and sugar and bring to a boil. Allow to cool. Add the orange juice and Kool-Aid mix. Pour into a freezer-safe container and store in the freezer until ready to serve.

To serve, chip the frozen slush with an ice pick. Put the slush pieces into a glass, filling about halfway. Fill the rest of the glass with soda, ginger ale, or champagne.

Makes 12 servings

Darla Gallo, Miss Darla
Capital Area Red Hatters,
Camp Hill, Pennsylvania

Instant Chai Tea Mix

1 cup nonfat dry milk	1½ cups unsweetened instant tea
1 cup non-dairy coffee creamer	2 teaspoons ground ginger
1 cup French vanilla non-dairy coffee creamer	2 teaspoons ground cinnamon
2½ cups sugar	1 teaspoon ground cloves

In a large bowl combine the dry milk, non-dairy creamer, vanilla non-dairy creamer, sugar, and instant tea. Stir in the ginger, cinnamon, and cloves. In a blender or food processor, blend 1 cup at a time, until the mixture is the consistency of fine powder.

To serve, stir 2 heaping tablespoons of the tea mixture into a mug of hot water. Store the dry mixture in an airtight container.

Makes 36 servings

Betty Anne Cloninger, Her Royal Highness,
Queen B, Goddess of Goodwill

Red Hat Hotties,
Dallas, North Carolina

Mama's Hot Cocoa

4 tablespoons unsweetened cocoa powder	2 tablespoons semisweet chocolate, shaved
2 to 3 tablespoons pure cane sugar	1 teaspoon vanilla (optional)
4 cups 1% or 2% milk	

In a 1-quart saucepan combine the cocoa powder and sugar. Mix well. Cook over medium and add the milk, whisking constantly. Add the chocolate. Bring to a boil, whisking constantly. When the sugar has dissolved, remove from the heat. Let stand for 2 minutes. Add vanilla, if desired.

Makes 2 servings

Sheri Dollar-Carpenter, HRM Sprinkles
Frayed Knots Mad Hatters,
Colfax, California

Fantastic Fiberglass Margaritas

1 (21-ounce) can frozen limeade	12 ounces tequila
1 (12-ounce) bottle 7-Up or Sprite	Ice
1 (12-ounce) bottle Mexican beer (other than Corona)	

In a blender mix the frozen limeade. Add the 7-Up, beer, and tequila. Fill the container with ice. Blend as desired. Serve as is, or freeze for 1 hour for frozen margaritas.

Makes 2 quarts

Sharon Ross, Queen Mother
Red Hat Vette Ladies,
Primm Springs, Tennessee

Sinful Eggnog

3 cups sugar
1 dozen large eggs, at room temperature, separated
1 cup whiskey
1 quart bourbon

1 cup dark rum
3 quarts whole milk
2 pints whipped cream, divided
Nutmeg

In a large bowl cream the sugar and egg yolks. Add the liquors and stir until light. Add the milk and beat well.

In a medium bowl beat the egg whites until stiff but not dry. Fold a large spoonful of the egg whites into the mixture using a slotted spoon. Fold in the remaining egg whites using the slotted spoon. Fold in 1 pint of the whipped cream. Just before serving, fold in the remaining 1 pint whipped cream, stirring constantly with a slotted spoon. The earlier ahead of serving time the eggnog is made, the smoother it becomes. Dust with nutmeg to serve.

Makes 3 quarts

Jetta Hanover, Jettapropulsion
Boa Babes,
Ocala, Florida

Contributor's Index

Recipe Index

Italics indicate pages with a photo.